WAR AT TEN ONWARDS

LEWIS CREEDON

authorHOUSE®

AuthorHouse™
1663 Liberty Drive
Bloomington, IN 47403
www.authorhouse.com
Phone: 1 (800) 839-8640

Published by AuthorHouse 02/12/2020

ISBN: 978-1-7283-4578-9 (sc)
ISBN: 978-1-7283-4577-2 (e)

Library of Congress Control Number: 2020902651

Print information available on the last page.

CHAPTER 1

The year 1939 was rather mixed for me and I suppose for most inhabitants of England, including my compatriots living along the south coast.

Being ten years old this was the big year when in March, you took an examination, on the recommendation of your school master, to see if there was enough spark in you to go to that educational Mecca, King Edward the Sixth School, Southampton, founded by the eponymous monarch in 1553 AD. Well there was, and I received handshakes from my benign schoolmaster, Mr. Marshall, and announcements at the school assembly of this hoped for, by my parents at least, a step up in the world. I was allowed to leave "ordinary" school until lunchtime to go home and convey the news to my mother, who of course always thought this would happen. I ran all the way home getting really out of breath on the way.

There followed a period of obtaining the appropriate uniform and equipment, a leather satchel for books from my aunt, the specified two kinds (!) of shoes and much other gear, some of it to a mandatory list. After that the year dragged on a bit, livened somewhat by the news that my best friend and fellow model aeroplane enthusiast was also on the list with me.

Then in August I got the mumps, a bizarre disease of no great importance which at one stage, fortunately only for a short period, makes your salivary glands swell up giving the impression of a singularly lucky chipmunk. Although confined to bed by mandate, I felt completely fit. One Sunday morning my Grandmother visited and since I could then hear reasonably well, from my upstairs bedroom I heard her say to my mother "He's started". Pretty significant words considering it was September the third.

Lying in bed I thought over the fact that I had heard that in the event of war the school was to be evacuated *en bloc* to somewhere else.

At the time the war was viewed as being equivalent to the destruction by bombing of the small town of Guernica in Spain, but spread over the entire country. The government had hundreds of thousands of cardboard coffins all ready, and we all had gas masks. They knew how destructive bombing could be but it was not for some four years that anybody really realised that aerial bombing was a colossal effort that at least at the beginning put all the bombs in ineffective places. (The process needed smartening up) Hence the dispersal of civilians to rural or industrially insignificant areas.

So I thought, "That does it, Hooray, they can't evacuate me I've got the mumps, the best thing that ever happened." Subsequent conversation with my mother firmly put paid to that idea, which had a short life in quite a few homes and resulted in a ragtag arrival of few evacuees at our destination in the next month or even year, of which I was to become one. Two quite remarkable late arrivals were John McAlpine, who wore a black tie instead of the school version. His father was ships doctor on the Athenia, sunk by a Uboat on the first day of the war. The other was Werner Goldberg, who spoke mainly German and who didn't have his parents with him.

So about three weeks into the war my mother took me on the train the vast distance of about thirty three miles from my home in Southampton to Poole, reducing the population around me from about 176,000 to 56,000. You might not think this to be significant if you cannot compare the two places.

Southampton where I started from was a port capable of handling any ship in the then world including the Queen Mary which was the largest. It had recently had a major refit. The port could service and repair most ships then at sea. It had cargo handling capacity which was the largest in Europe and more than ample warehousing including a major cold store. From my bedroom window I could actually watch the Queen Mary enter the largest dry dock in the world for her annual overhaul. A truly wonderful target.

Poole was also a port. The largest vessel it could handle was probably 3000 tons, a strategically insignificant size. It had however a very large harbour, roughly two and a half miles square and later to be recognised (not by the Germans) as being very, very useful. It was and is a very pleasant town where I don't think I ever had a negative experience although one or two were highly dangerous. My mother and I went by train to Poole and were shunted through the school, Poole Grammar School, which had a syllabus comparable to King Edwards but not the prestige, thence to the Municipal buildings from whence we were directed to my home for the next two years in St. Marys Road.

The house was a neat well maintained traditional English three bedroom bungalow. It's owners Mr. & Mrs. B. were nice and of a type to benignly impress their standards on me for ever. They, poor folks, had to take what evacuees came since they had spare rooms, so a certain amount of courage was needed on their part. I hope to this day I did not call on it. After a strange handing over my mother walked off down the road to the station while I watched through the window, trying to hide tears.

My host, (host and hostess were the mandatory nomenclature) was a skilled carpenter of 37, a trade unionist, branch secretary (unpaid), and choirman at the Parkstone Congregational Church, which has left me with a lifelong appreceation for religious music since I was more or less compelled to attend choir practice and church or be left home alone. Not in wartime! His wife (a mere housewife!) was also in the choir. By my standards at the time their house was luxurious, they had some lovely Poole pottery which I have since collected myself and a piano, and most important a feeling of comfort. I found out years later that they were involuntarily childless.

Surprisingly none of the above events were actively imposed by Germany, this was the so called "phoney" war. (The etymology of that word escapes me.) Lord Gort and our solidly ill equipped troops trundled across the channel with their shovels and bayonets and precious little else, fully prepared to start again where they had left off in 1918.

Poole harbour is nearly cut of from the sea by a substantial sand bar, imaginatively called Sandbanks, a piece of real estate priced to match Manhatten and from the declaration until the war actually began this was a delightful nearly deserted beach. A member of my class had a father, locally employed, who undertook voluntarily to teach his son and anyone else who came along to swim there. Regrettably my course was interrupted by events, never to be resumed. In passing, it was customary when you got the scholarship to receive a bicycle and this enabled me to go anywhere within perhaps fifteen miles, and Sandbanks was only five.

Then the trouble started. Both Poole and Southampton are about seventy miles from the French coast where the Germans turned up in May and June. It was apparent that Britannia had better rule at least the waves in earnest. Recreational Sandbanks initially became deserted. I still cycled there because it was a nice place but the lack of company was very obvious. There were events that made a considerable impression. I was one day digging a tunnel into the side of a big sand dune when there was a loud bang and the tunnel fell in and buried my arm. (It was small diameter tunnel.) I rushed to the top of the sand dune and looked towards the harbour mouth to see a large cloud of spray and/or steam and what looked like the bottom of a vessel. No confirmation in the press of course but I had heard that a Heinkel seaplane was about laying mines from the air at night. Something of a waste, there were much bigger vessels to the east at that time.

Troops began to appear at Sandbanks, one day I had the enlightening experience of watching bayonet practice, a truly educational experience for a young lad. You have to put your foot on the body sometimes to get the bayonet out.

There was a chain ferry which ran across the harbour mouth to the Studland road, but normal people, unless they had a car or bike usually took "Davises Boats" which consisted of one 20ft. open boat with a diesel engine and was much more fun. At this time it stopped its competitive ferry job and went to Dunkirk where it ferried troops from the beach to larger ships. It resumed work with small commemorative brass plate after the war.

The teaching program at school was very different from the peacetime one, since two complete schools were in residence in one building. The arrangement was admirable. On one week one of the schools started classes at 8.45am and finished at 12.45 pm, 4 hours on six (!) days per week, nearly the normal 25 hour week. The other school started in the afternoon at 1.15pm and worked until 5.15 pm the exact equivalent. At the end of each week the schools switched times and never the twain met. The V.I.P.s neat trick was that Poole Grammer School kept their desks holding their books, which we were in honor bound not to open, and we had specially imported lockers in the equivalent classrooms. I never heard of an illicit transfer of goods in five years. The mornings were of little use due to the need to lunch before 11.30 and were mostly confined to dull activities like homework, although I did visit the library (P.G.Wodehouse especially and Richmal Crompton) certainly not in search of erudition.

The afternoons were different. We could easily visit places within five miles and even ten at a push. I used to go sometimes to Bournemouth if I was a bit homesick, a good ride to get a Southampton newspaper which was printed there.

A result of this arrangement was that one weekend we would be free from Saturday lunch to Monday lunch and on alternate weekends from Saturday evening to Monday morning and this, in spite of the perceived dangers, allowed us to go back to Southampton for two nights on the correct weekend. Until June 1940 we certainly did not perceive any danger and by then, when the random and thinly spread bombing began to thicken up, we were pretty set in our ways. In hindsight, until the bombers were radar & pathfinder directed, very few raids were actually raids, being little more than random scatterings, as a few unfortunate villages and farm animals found out. This counter intuitive return weekend made use of the train service of course. The logical relevant train times were 2.24 pm to Southampton and 10.29am to return to Poole but schoolboys with characteristic ingenuity found out that there was an earlier train to Southampton at 12.44 pm on Saturdays, a difficult one minute anamoly.

It was discovered that by running like the devil you could leave school at 12.45p.m. and actually catch the 12.44, a sort of reverse time travel. The solution was progressive. Firstly the boys left a minute or two early while their master either unintentionally or in collusion looked the other way. Then the station staff, having noticed some breathless schoolboys on a regular Saturday basis, failed to start the train on time and the final resolution was that the headmaster altered the quitting time to 12.30p.m. for that Saturday only. A very distant result is that anybody reading this should not be confused if the tale wanders between the two main locations, Southampton and

Poole. The events moved between the two locations virtually every two weeks.

Reverting to Sandbanks the chain ferry was kept going right through the war but access to the beach was cut off. I still cycled to Sandbanks because "The Haven" at the tip of the peninsula was an interesting place to watch boats, cars and people. The boats were significant at the time of Dunkirk not because they brought soldiers back from the beaches, since that run was too far, but any little freighter from the other side of the channel was likely to have a few rather desolate but almost invariably very well dressed people standing on deck for their first glimpse of a fortunately continued life.

One day, cycling back to Poole from Sandbanks I presumably got too deeply into thought and cycled at a plodding speed into the back of a stationary car. There was no other traffic and I <u>was</u> "deep in thought". My bike however was slightly and irretrievably bent but still completely functional. On the subject of bicycles, Ted Clarke my friend at that time of two years standing, had to change the worn brake blocks on his bike. He replaced them with wartime blocks and on a run down the rather long Constitution Hill they melted, fortunately without fatal results.

It was about this time that I had an interesting and dangerous experience while under the impression that it was only interesting. The local anti aircraft guns were like everybody else very aware of Guernica and were not about to allow that to happen to us. For the first but certainly not for the last time, as we were walking home from church one Sunday in the dark they opened up with a terrific series of explosions. We walked on, huddled together and felt comforted by the thought that we were well defended. After some small interval we heard noises as if some boys were throwing stones up in the air. It took a little while to realise that we were being rained with shell splinters, some with known masses of a half pound all of which had fallen at least two thousand feet. We got home allright, in a similar event in London, presumably on a larger scale the death score was Germans 0 (actually there were none present), civilians 14.

In Southampton at this time my father was installing the government supplied Anderson Shelter, which owed nothing at all to the eponymous Sir

John Anderson, the Home Secretary at the time of its inception. As a person later involved in earthy engineering I have to say it was a superb design for whom no credit was given to anyone, it is worth a description in case of an accidental atomic war. It was put together from pieces of corrugated steel just under one tenth of an inch thick, corrugated at 2" depth at about 8" pitch and held together with 5/8 inch bolts. The body was straight at the sides and was curved at the top to form half an an arch some seven feet high, the pair five feet wide and there were corrugated end plates. The arch pieces were about two feet wide and lapped over so that the shelter could be built in increments of two feet. The normal length was eight feet. It was designed to be buried to a depth of three feet and the excavated earth was to be piled on top of the arches. My father decided it could be buried to four feet deep with the aid of a stepdown, giving a lot more earth to go on top. He not only installed ours, a considerable labor but also a second one for my aunt and grandmother. I would mention that the first of a stick of four bombs fell about five feet alongside the second of his shelters, stripped the earth from that side and the top and leaned the arch sideways by about two feet. My aunt and grandmother were inside, completely unharmed.

The second of that stick hit the back of the house opposite ours. I wanted to go round there to look at the damage... my mother, significantly said no!

The third bomb of that stick also created a story since it didn't explode. All three bombs were small probably no more than 100 kilogrammes. The appropriate soldiery arrived to get rid of it. The ground was very soft clay and these poor soldiers dug a deeper and deeper hole for perhaps a week while the area was fenced off and the bomb sank deeper as they dug. They couldn't get under it. The hole had to be shored up with timber to keep it open. The decision was eventually made to explode it in situ. It was about four feet from a house which was obviously going to be damaged, but there was little alternative. The people who lived there were allowed to remove all their possessions which they did, I imagine hurriedly, and the police went round the area telling everyone that at four o'clock the device would be exploded. "Stay indoors and away from windows..." Both my house and Ted Clark's house were in the designated area and I was visiting him as we were building a model aeroplane. His mother dragged a mattress into the living room and put it on edge round the dining table legs and at five to four we got under the table, quite a crowd.

The bang was typical and not too earth shattering, it was the subsequent shower of mud and timber shoring that had the real effect and was unexpectedly noisy. Ted's mother had bedsheets on her clothesline drying and the mud stains lasted the life of the sheets! The housebricks bore the stain for forty years. Real clay! The timber made excellent firewood and I found large bomb fragments.

Another event in our street was when an incendiary bomb landed on a semidetached house opposite ours. It lodged in the guttering (these bombs had braking fins) and fizzed away in the usual manner. Had a ladder been available it could have been easily dislodged, there wasn't one so two homes were destroyed.

My father did a rather interesting thing about this time, A bank had been bombed and he brought home several pennies he found. It was technically looting. The penalty was death!!

Poole was being revised. What was obviously a tank defence line was being established. It involved Poole Park Lake, the railway line which enclosed it and a variety of natural features intended to delay any enemy advance pending obliteration, not that there were many anti tank weapons available. A lot of this involved insitu cast concrete blocks of over a cubic yard in a line enclosing the beach. It was necessary in places to leave gaps in this line for daily access and at this point there was often an old car filled with sand which could be pushed into the opening. I never saw an anti tank gun, I reckon they were spread very thinly.

There was no conceivable reason to bomb Poole at this time but a couple did land a hundred yards or so from where I lived. (my billet?) It is interesting to speculate that if you were flying in marginal visibility the large expanse of water stretching inland, which Poole Harbor represented could be mistaken for

Southampton, in which case the two bombs which landed nearby would have hit potentially valuable targets. They got my attention at least. One hit the hotel/restaurant "The Shah of Persia" and left it a beacon of flame. (I visited recently and none of the staff knew about it.) The other landed on open land and made a neat crater about 40 ft. diameter with uniformly sloping sides. This, of course, was used as a perfectly banked cycle track by the youth of the area, and is now a small bungalow.

About this time my school, my parents and my hosts decided that I had better change digs. I never had any explanation for this, or much else, come to that. So without malice I moved a little further from school to Wimborne Road, curiously un-numbered. Here lived a fellow evacuee, George Groves from the middle of Southampton, a year younger than me and compatible. We both liked aeroplanes.

Our new hostess was, to us, a "very old" widow of sixty three who turned out to be a bit of a sport, quite capable of passing the cigarettes around, having a niece who lived in Stenhurst Road with her charming daughter Molly who interested me strangely (at least that's what I thought at the time). My friend Ted lived a mile or so up the road in Broadstone in a large house with three unmarried sisters. He moved eventually to Constitution Hill in Poole as a result of strange events. A great deal of tension was apparent in that household and it transpired that one of the sisters was pregnant from undefined cause, resulting in dinner plates being thrown about (with dinner). Hence the move to Constitution Hill. Life however continued in its loosely defined way.

I had at least two interesting events on my way home from school. There was, one day a mess in the middle of the street consisting of a white powder and some pieces of metal. I identified it as the remains of an incendiary bomb which had burned itself out. Somebody, whom I resent to this day, had taken the braking fin which stopped it falling fast enough to smash itself to useless small pieces. The principal residue was a lot of white powder. Since this was Milk of Magnesia in its purest form I dipped my finger in it and licked it off. There were no perceptible consequences.

The other interesting event was that I found a recently discarded banana skin! If you think this is trivial, just remember nobody in England had seen a banana for three years! But that is another story.

My interest in aeroplanes was given a large amount of subject matter while in Poole. Firstly and most conspicuously the Harbour being very large was an ideal place for seaplanes. There was an extremely active flying boat training base which used Supermarine Walrus biplane amphibians based in a large yacht servicing hangar in Sandbanks. That aircraft is extremely noisy and the landing approach often was over the school resulting in a temporary hiatus in lessons. Even worse, if there was a northerly component in the wind the take off path was near the school. There was also a biplane floatplane, a Fairey Seafox which had two floats and also astonishingly a triple float, radial engined Chance Vought Kingfisher trainer. And that was just the training establishment based in Sandbanks! I don't know if the Catalina flying boats also present were actually on antisubmarine patrol duty or training.

The yacht club at Lilliput was completely separate and rather intriguing but you had to be very observant to notice what went on, since it merely operated launches. These went out to the visiting Short "C" class airliners which were civilian planes which, as far as I know mostly visited via Lisbon the Middle east and South Africa, even possibly the far east. It was on one of these flights that Leslie Howard was shot down and killed.

The aircraft that was most important, although we didn't know it at the time, was the very large Boeing 314 A. Like most large flying boats at the time it was built in the belief that the world lacked enough aerodromes. If you were Winston Churchill or head of the Imperial General Staff or some such person, you would fly in one of those to Lisbon, the Caribbean and Florida. The V.I.P.s came from London, stayed overnight at the Royal Bath Hotel in Bournemouth (nothing but the best) then to Lilliput and via Boeing

314 A to see the President. On one or two occasions an Airspeed Ensign flew over for no conceivable reason except possibly pilot curiosity and only once a Ju.88. Southampton at that time experienced the best night bombing raid the Germans could manage i.e. the bombs fell pretty much where intended. No radar was needed. Their intentions were erroneous. They knew that Southampton was at the junction of two rivers, so they bombed that. What they did not realise was that this was a commercial area. Shops by the hundred were destroyed, but very little else. My aunt, who worked in a downtown department store went to work one morning and could not find the store. She was unable to find the street either! Supermarine Works were not damaged, neither were the ship repair facilities nor the docks except by odd strays.

Having decided, presumably by reconnaissance that they got it wrong, they did the only possible but very expensive thing for them... mount daylight raids. These were very accurate and were virtually part of the "Battle of Britain". Supermarine works were virtually wrecked, somewhat late as everything vital had already been shifted to over thirty different locations within thirty miles only one of which, a car dealership in Southampton, received so much as an unimportant near miss.

I witnessed one daylight raid which was reasonably successful, or damaging depending on your point of view. There was that day a cloud base of about three thousand feet and just below it following the line of the New Dock wall was a Junkers 88. There was a lot anti aircraft fire, the sky peppered with puffs of smoke which the pilot ignored, obviously intent on his target and holding a straight course. They all appeared to miss, there was no visible effect. One of the planes gunners had the infernal cheek to shoot our local barrage balloon down in flames. The plane flew out of sight. I heard from my father that evening that he was targeting the docks and scored a direct hit on the large cold storage facility which burned. The dock eventually was running in butter! That sort of thing was worrying. Lots of noise & we felt like spectators. There was an anti aircraft gun on the cold storage roof, and the crew were stranded up there. My father volunteered to go on to the roof by crane as did a few others. He wasn't chosen being a bit older. The fellow who went up there got the George Medal.

In August 1940 I was home for the annual School Holiday of about a month. Thus I saw quite a bit of action. It consisted mostly of vapor trails, high up intertwining figures on most occasions, other times the trails were short. It was not really possible to follow the action although there was plenty of it. The significance of the one outstanding piece of action I saw was explained to me some fifty years later by one of my working colleagues who made extensive studies of the air activity of that period and was a modeller, up to the point of having models on exhibition in the Smithsonian. What I saw was two parachutes about the same height, probably about five thousand feet, descending normally, if such a description can be applied. I heard later that one landed about three quarters of a mile from my house and some sort of fist fight took place!

The long delayed explanation was that one parachute carried a wounded German pilot and the other a wounded Flight Lieutenant Nicholson. Flt.Lt. Nicholson had shot down the German when himself wounded and in his burning Spitfire. The altercation occurred amongst the Home guard, under orders to shoot at any more than two parachutes. Someone thought thought it was wrong to shoot at wounded men or in this case at all. They missed anyway. The Flt. Lt. was awarded the only Victoria Cross of the Battle of Britain. My Grandmother, who was in charge that morning ordered me back in to the shelter.

To the north of Poole at that time there was a very large expanse of heathland stretching up to Tolpuddle. When the Stukas first, appeared over France they were seen to be a very effective weapon. It was not realised at the time that they were easy prey for fighters, and it was clear that we had no such weapon. The result was that the Westland Lysander was quickly adapted to one of its original design goals and set about training on the above heath as a dive bomber. Most intriguing from my viewpoint they dived steeply behind a rise in the ground before pulling out. I don't think they were ever used in that role. The heath had other uses. Live fire exercises were conducted amid distant explosions and tanks roamed the heath. I was never aware of any limitation on access to these areas which I often visited. My friend Roy Pomeroy discovered a heap of .303 rifle ammunition which had been run over by a tank, so in accordance with the contemporary schoolboy ethic he pocketed a fair sampling. (Didn't we all?) Later by way of experiment he put a complete round on to a small fire. The bullet penetrated his abdomen in the region of his appendix and a girl I knew helped him walk home with the bullet in him. The doctors took out his appendix "for an encore".

My first "host" worked as a carpenter (as wartime directed labour) in a factory at Holton Heath which was engaged in producing amongst other things 4.7" AA shells and 20mm. aircraft cannon munitions. Blanks for the AA shells were delivered to Holton Heath by rail and were trucked to the factory on inadequate looking vehicles, three wheeled tugs with two wheeled trailers, right past my billet. Sometimes bits of the cargo fell off (really!) and in this way I acquired a 20 mm. live head cannon shell. I kept it for a while but Pom's experience with a comparatively miniature munition induced me to bury it. Some forty years later it was no longer there.

However there was a good chance of survival if you confined yourself to .303" bullets. The thing to do with these was to take the bullet out of the cartridge, stand the cartridge upright on a piece of slate and set fire to the cordite contents. This produced a bright flame for about a minute, followed by by a sharp crack as the spent case rode 100 feet into the air and the copper percussion cap drilled through the slate and three inches into the underlying soil.

The cissy thing to to was to remove the cordite sticks, arrange them on a piece of wood and burn your initials into it. Another thing, desirable but only rarely obtainable, was the Thunderflash. This was designed to make a very loud but harmless noise for battle training purposes. What you must understand is that these dangerous objects were all boys treasures and conferred status on their owners. If you could have acquired a 1000lb. bomb you would probably have become King.

My friend Brian Turvey while on vacation in Southampton, got a twisted intestine needing an operation. He died of the consequent infection. No penicillin.

Not all hostesses were what one might hope for, mine for instance sometimes passed round the cigarettes. Another kept her lad up late playing Monopoly when he wasn't well. Didn't help his polio. One had a husband in the forces but took in young men! I'm sure there were others. Mine also had a niece about a mile away who had a pretty daughter who visited evenings after her shorthand lesson. I had to walk her home for which I was a bit young, but we did hold hands. Not to mention Ted Clarke's three sisters in Broadstone.

My mother visited about the time the Germans got to the French coast. We went to Bournemouth and went up the East Cliff near the Royal Bath Hotel. From there we had an excellent view of the Royal Engineers who were demolishing the pier with explosives. Once again lots of timber flying up in the air and loud bangs. About this time three very tall masts appeared on the top of the Purbeck Hills. They were a vital part of the South Coast radar chain, and partly covered for Ventnor when it was bombed out for a short while. It was believed they were never suspected by the Germans, they were very hard to see since they were so slender.

When our school arrived in Poole there had been very little time for preparation. This was slowly made up for. Firstly air raid shelters were dug, some near the school, but in view of the large numbers others were five minutes vulnerable walk away! They consisted of boarded trenches, quite deep and covered with about two feet of earth. They had a problem in that when a couple of classrooms of boys shuffled through them the dust was virtually opaque, with concomitant breathing and seeing problems. Fortunately they were not much used being replaced by the "brick box" type early on. The other improvement was viewed with much less enthusiasm by the pupils. Two houses were acquired, Ledgard House and Seldown House, both since "developed". This enabled two of our half days to be filled with lessons. Definitely retrograde!

Something which at this length of time I still find hard to account for was the attendance of a small group including myself at a dance at the Centenary Hall, (I didn't know anyone, including myself who could dance). It was presumably "oversubscribed" since we never did get in nor did a group of sailors standing frustrated at the entrance. One sailor in the group said to another, "Are you from the Turtle?" The reply was apparently unsatisfactory since the interrogator punched the respondent so hard he landed in the middle of the street. There were probably inter ship wars superimposed on the larger pattern.

We did other innocent things. My friend Godfrey Cawte and I decided that the twenty five foot sandstone cliff at Whitecliff (no reason at all for the name) which at that time was practically vertical, offered an excellent opportunity to cut steps and climb since we had read a few Alpine books. We obtained a perfect iron spike to dig with and set to work. This attracted a small amount of attention amongst our friends and we were about ten feet up when one of these friends visited. He tried the first ten feet and the cliff face with him on it departed its station, leaving him unharmed, covered with sandstone and sand, lying on his back on the beach, fortunately soft sand. We were annoyed, it set us back about two weeks! We set to work to repair the damage, cutting replacement steps in better quality sandstone until we were very near the top. It was evident that we could cut no further steps in the crumbley 45 degree slope which constituted the last three feet, so we went home. I happened down that way a day or so later, I looked at it and decided it was fit to climb. I succeeded and as the clay crumbled under my feet stepped to the top. I simultaneously decided that it was utterly unsafe and totally foolish. I met Godfrey the next day and told him. In spite of his considerable investment in the project I think he saw that I was thoroughly scared and so agreed. We took out the lower few steps. Today that has eroded to a scrubby, mild slope with bushes, the name Whitecliff is even less appropriate.

We weren't all stupid all the time. The school collected salvage for the war effort, one courageous group pushed an old Morgan three wheeler two miles to the scrap heap! And we collected astonishing amounts of paper!

There were other more or less violent incidents. One day I was, as usual on my bike, riding past the Municipal Buildings in Poole, looking into the Park across the cricket ground when there was a loud explosion on the other side of the field accompanied by the customary cloud of earth and mud. A bomb had landed with no warning whatsoever and blown up the tiny park zoo, killing the monkey. No warning, no sirens, just an impromptu bang.

It transpired that there was an undetected German aircraft above the broken cloud. Apparently he had spotted a Boeing 314A coming in to land on an unusual E.W. approach and had taken appropriate action. The sirens went later.

My last encounter (second hand) with violence was when a crippled JU88 flew low over Upper Parkstone and crashed in the northern reaches of Poole. In a rather ghoulish manner I cycled to the crash site in the hope of souvenirs. I found a piece of obviously tubular control rod made of aluminium, However I mistook it for drain pipe and left it! I found out later that one off the crew had bailed out at low altitude and landed on the roof of the pottery in Upper Parkstone sans parachute. I still marvel at the callous insensitivity of the youth of which I was a member.

An intriguing event was the arrival of foreign troops. We had some French ones near us but I, at least, lacked the courage to embark on schoolboy French. Their English was limited but I believe to this day that they made the best coffee in the world. Theirs was a very courageous position after being "defeated".

Next there were the Americans. We often had to join in the softball games which we enjoyed I believe more than the Americans, very little standing about and much noise. I continued playing softball until about 1950 with other English afficionados, the equipment was inherited. We also found out there were regional Americans, just imagine, real Mexicans!

There is in Branksome in one of the more jungly areas a footpath suspension bridge across the "chine". Our use for it was to try to set up a resonant oscillation. You couldn't get it more than three or four degrees out of kilter which was always a disappointment. If you have read Winston Churchill's youthful memorabilia you will know he stayed with relatives nearby and played here. One day in an attempt to avoid his "enemies", he jumped from this bridge into a tree which he intended to climb down and "get away". Unfortunately he missed the tree and ended up in hospital.

One day during a German lesson a very unusual aircraft circled over Poole Harbour. I could not recognise it neither could the local anti aircraft gunners. They responded with the utmost effort. The noise, which seems to figure largely in warfare, was once again very loud. It was a floatplane appropriately enough but it only did two circuits and left. The utterly stupid schoolboy response was to rush to the very large window for the best possible view. Our German teacher, a wounded veteran of the Somme, enjoined us in the loudest voice of which he was capable to get away from the large expanse of glass. Nobody was hurt except possibly our poor schoolmaster at the sight of so many idiot schoolboys. There was of course no press coverage but it transpired that, in conformance with the belief that the world lacked airfields two (only) Spitfires had been given floats. This was the second improved one, piloted by Jeffrey Quill. He said later that he wasn't frightened of the guns, if they could not recognise a Spitfire after three years of war they obviously weren't sharp enough to shoot him down.

By about April 1944 it was obvious that something unusual was about to happen so I did a lot of cycling to examine the symptoms. The furthest was to Holmsley Airfield, half way back to Southampton, converted from a very large open heath to an airfield with long crossed runways and many aircraft standing spots. American B24 bombers (Liberators), not too remarkable in wartime, were scattered about in large numbers. One had its elegant high aspect ratio "Davis" wing stretching about 20 feet across the A35 highway, badly parked but high up!

Much more active was Somerford Aerodrome in Christchurch which was a base for P 47 Thunderbolt fighters being used at the time as locomotive busters in France. When I was there hanging on the fence they seemed to operate in a continuous stream, I saw one return with a damaged wing (standing right under their flight path!!) There were several gaps in the hedge at the approach, east, end of the field, presumably the result of "short landings". It was a very small airfield, originally belonging to Airspeed who made "Oxford" trainers and post war the "Ambassador" airliner. I got to know this airfield better later. Much, much later it consists of small bungalows.

My furthest ride was to Tarrant Rushton airfield. As far as I could see it had only one runway. If there were more they would not have been visible to me since, from the top of an overlooking hill all that could be seen were "Horsa" gliders and their tugs, Albemarles and D C 3's, at least a hundred aircraft. It was quite clear what was about to happen. The field appeared to be paved with aircraft.

During this period the whole of South coast was cut off from the rest of the country by *fiat*, and by good fortune I was inside this banned area and could move freely.

Operating the usual school travel cycle, I was in Southampton during this time and was absolutely astonished at the scene. All the roads leading towards the docks and some portion of all the adjacent side roads were filled with American army trucks. I also saw a very large convoy of trucks labelled as the "Red Ball Express". It was an entirely black personell transport group, apparently devoted to feeding the front line with munitions. Large locomotives were being loaded *down ramps* on to ships, which to a railway enthusiast like myself is inconceivable. (Locomotives are only flexible in the horizontal plane) Apparently the Thunderbolts had done a complete job.

And the streets of Southampton were draped with wires connected to what could have been waste containers. Fortunately this system was not required but had enemy aircraft appeared the entire area would have vanished in an enormous cloud of synthetic fog, and specific targets would have been undetectable. Presumably all the enemy aircraft were in Russia because they didn't turn up.

I was in Poole on June 6th. I woke up at the usual time to the sound of many aircraft. The sound of aero engines continued until about ten o'clock. The cloud base was probably two thousand feet and most of the planes were below it and heading south.

By now I was old enough to stop being a spectator so I joined the Air Training Corps in Westbourne. I may say that at first this was incredibly boring, at least the Morse code bit which practically constituted the whole effort. (I'm still not too good at it.) The drill was not excessively unpleasant and was enlightened by one of our number who arrived independently at the decision that when you started to march you simultaneously advanced both your left leg and your left arm. He also had a little trouble with right and left. We had a real disappointment, which may not sound much but was very upsetting, particularly as I turned out to be the most aeronautical of my squad. We were scheduled one Sunday for a flight, my first, at Somerford aerodrome ten miles away. By this time the Thunderbolts were in France and I don't suppose Somerford figured largely in the battle plans. I put on my hot thick uniform and enthusiastically cycled ten miles through the rain, slowly becoming wet sponge like. The Avro Anson had a flat tire needing repair, which we would have to wait for. After a two hour wait in soggy uniform in a bare unheated requisitioned bungalow we were told the aircraft was unserviceable. We didn't even see it! I cycled home, also in continuous rain.

There was one good thing. I was a complete and total aircraft recognition nut. I knew every relevant and irrelevant aircraft in the war from Spitfire through to the Henschel 125 and Savoia Marchetti 72 and Northrop A17A. My squad, about 30 lads, were divided into two teams for a recognition contest. My team won, the score was 33 to 3 and I got 30 of them. Inevitably you can't lose them all.

I was finally checked out of the Air Training Corps by an officer I had not previously met and left Poole with a few token High Jinks. I much regretted never having seen a V1. However one day shortly after our return to Southampton I was cycling up the Avenue when I saw parked at the side of the road a large trailer carrying a complete V2 rocket! I was able to have a good look at it, including its ingenious combustion system, now commonplace.

CHAPTER 2

At the end of the war the school returned to Southampton. As you can imagine we were returning to circumstances of which we had no prior knowledge. Home was fairly easy since we had diluted experience of this right through the war. The new school year was however spectacularly different, larger modern buildings and I myself to a newer and slightly more academic atmosphere, the "Lower Sixth."

This needs a little explanation. You may have guessed that my family, with six children of which I was the eldest did not carry much in the way of social status and while I was anxious to get into the aircraft industry my elders and betters regarded that my being in the sixth form at K.E.S raised the whole tone of the neighbourhood. So on I went, losing the advantage of skipping the first year of part time study as an apprentice due to my "classical" studies not to mention the year late start. Interesting and laying on a very thin veneer of classical knowledge. You leave many people behind but go up the wrong road.

However there were model planes to build, speedboats etc. not to mention feeble attempts at jet engines and setting off our munition built victory banger, not to mention our first proper model flying. Amongst other things I built a six feet span model glider, my little sister punctured every one of the tissue covered panels in the wing.

I was inveigled, by my friend Ted Clarke into joining the church youth club which had GIRLS, which I hadn't really noticed much before, (except for my sister who doesn't count) this enlivened the dull moment and cheered the tedious hour. Ach wie viel ich mich begluckt. I happened at this time to fall heavily for a girl at the end of our road, so I wrote her an innocent note which was intercepted by her mother. I received a public rebuke in the street from her mother. I was embarrassed. A few days later her father invited me in to their house to show me their home movies, when the mother was out of course.

Education comes in strange ways. Much later the girl married a classmate of mine at King Edwards.

Reality however was about to set in. My application to Supermarine for employment as an apprentice was accepted and I was invited for interview. I got the impression that I was welcome, matriculation exemption and all. Forty seven hour week, 6d an hour (10c at the time), one day off per week during term time for technical studies at Southampton University, start next Monday at Sunlight Laundry!!! Which needs a little explanation. Supermarine Works building, which was quite small was bombed early in the war and very quickly was made to spread like a virus to over 30 locations in Southern England and a large shadow factory near Birmingham. I was interviewed by a large man who didn't seem to operate with much interest and told me that my aeromodelling enthusiasm was irrelevant. Mr. Lennox Taylor who conducted the interview was a few months later found guilty of molesting small boys and sent to jail for six months. But I was about to join the organization that built 22,000 Spitfires and distinguished itself and I didn't know this or care when I found out.

Sunlight Laundry was a shop devoted to putting together sub assemblies of various sizes which were sent to a place where they were assembled into large pieces of aeroplane and thence to every apprentices ambition, final assembly. This was part of a continuous stream converting raw material to aeroplanes. There were interspersed among this stream specialists who for various reasons could not be moved around the country who did magic tricks. It is worth describing one of these in detail. He could take a 15 inch square of thin sheet metal, fold it on itself across a diagonal such that the fold line was a <u>curve</u>. This made the balance horn for the Spitfire's rudder, and on the face of it is impossible, which is the class of work roughly that skilled workers do for a living. Finished parts were marked with their part number and added to the storekeepers stock, to be issued on demand for further assembly. Factories work in general by such means.

Just as a point of interest when I got home on the first day I fell asleep for two hours, industry is appropriately named.

My model aeroplane friend Ted happened to notice that the part numbering operative was a truly spectacular redhead, and he was frowned upon for allowing this to distract him. Our big blustering chargehand did not however receive admonition for expounding on the delights of married life, but later acquired a daughter.

My school friend Ken Whitmarsh, in my class at school but a year ahead of me at work due to my sixth form adventure, one day came across from the bus station next door (also known as the wing shop) to ask how I was getting on. We chatted for a minute and I asked him what work he was doing. I got my first introduction to refined shop language when he replied "buggerall."

My next door neighbour at home also worked "on the bench" at Sunlight and she derived satisfaction, evidenced by a smirk, at the sight of "the sixth form boy" in overalls.

It was about this time that the work week was reduced to 40 hours which abolished Saturday, morning working as the norm for ever.

I had a few months of this, useful and interesting because, in spite of what the apprentice supervisor asserted, model aircraft so far appeared to follow full scale inmost respects. I then had a session of the most boring time I believe of my entire working life. A group of about four of us were transferred to Eastleigh Airport flight shed, our instructions were to tidy it up. We were ensconced in there for about four weeks with virtually nothing to do, just an occasional visit from authority. There were however a few interesting circumstances, outside this monster flight shed was was parked a real Grumman Marauder, an impressive twin engined American bomber. In the interest of education it was carefully examined by us. Since no such plane had ever been stationed at Eastleigh we assumed that at the late stage of the war it had malfunctioned and made a precautionary landing. It was still there when we left but we heard later that it was cut up for scrap. Sic transit gloria belli.

The works canteen was about a quarter mile from our flight shed if you crossed the airfield diagonally, one day a group of us had to run very hard to avoid being hit by a landing Fairey Barracuda, good food however! And never a word of admonition!

Eventually I was relieved to be shifted to the main hangar where I was subject to the massive indignity of shortening thousands of tiny rivets which were used to attach Viking airliner fin skins which were being built in that shop. They got the right size eventually.

Surely by way of atonement a fellow apprentice and I were given a "Spiteful" rudder to skin on our own (being slyly watched from a distance.) One suspects the influence of our new apprentice supervisor. Sunny days! AND we did it properly.

I was moved across the shop floor then to the REAL workplace, the sheet metal section-head Jack Rolf, second in command maestro Cyril Russell, survivor of the Southampton bombing, sometime Chief Ratefixer at Follands, and a man who could form a Spitfire cowling in 45 minutes for which the official time was eight (!) hours. I make no great claim to skill but when Cyril has finished with you, you certainly know enough to start learning. My achievement was to make a tricky part for the tip of the Viking fin. His books are amusing and instructive. And you began to think that perhaps your job wasn't silly after all.

There was a considerable disadvantage in working at Eastleigh, at least for cyclists. Firstly the route was hilly, all right in the morning but not so good after work, and it rained! You could be soggy all day and wetter going home, six miles each way.

A very big advantage from my point of view was that some final assembly and checkout was done at Eastleigh, so I saw Spitfires in all states of assembly, engine run, and finally fly away to the real checkout field, usually Chilbolton.

There is a cautionary tale here. Len Gooch, a big wheel in the company, was standing in the middle of the hangar, well suited and lord of his domain when Dickie Barrell walked by carrying an awkward armful of parts. Now Dickie was an "elderly apprentice" having piloted a Halifax bomber, getting himself shot out of the sky with an injured hand and parachuting into Germany when he should have been apprenticing. Poor Dickie accidentally dropped a few things on the floor and Len Gooch was publicly somewhat critical. Remarks like, "He was flying a bomber when you were supervising a lot of bloody girls" were made. Careful! Gooch later got the O.B.E. for his war service.

About this *time* our improved apprentice supervisor arranged talks for bunch of us by the Chief Planner of the company, laying out the entire operation of the company from the gleam in the customers eye to delivery and from this moment for the first time I felt I knew what I was doing. Quite remarkable and very useful. There is a great deal of invisible detail. Naively I didn't really think about where I was to be moved next and it was a great shock to me to be told it was Newbury, a place of which I was completely ignorant, and hoped to remain so.

It was however a treasure of a works, literally all kinds of equipment, machine tools, automatic, semi-automatic and human, a five thousand ton rubber press which could make dozens of sheet metal smaller partsper second, heat treatment, the whole bit.

Nothing is ever perfect, we had four nights a week in lodgings and a train journey each week end to home and the arbitrary one day at Southampton University, fortunately expenses paid. Criminal elements among the apprentices bought return tickets, Southampton-Eastleigh and Newbury-Highclere thus avoiding paying for the bit in between. One knew of this but didn't split. nearby Highclere Castle, later known as Downton Abbey we never saw. More adventurous people even hitch hiked.

Shaw Works was one large building set on the top of a hill, overlooking open country largely composed of fields with classic English hedgerows.

In the course of lunchtime exploration we (the apprentices} discovered that every six feet or so in these hedges there was a chaffinch nest with eggs. Slight ornithological mystery!

My chargehand, Arthur Shaw (the works was not named after him) was good man who set out to make something of his apprentices. I would say that learned skill or not, one certainly understood the problems due to his efforts. My first tool was a shaper, a cutting tool was moved to and fro and as it did so it shaved metal as required off the workpiece. (Don't get in the way) I met with his approval and was shifted to surface grinder, thence thence to a Ward 2A capstan lathe suitable for mass production of small parts. My most difficult job was on the shaper where I had to make a lever which operated the differential braking on a Spitfire. When I eventually "grew up" I realised it was difficult because a poor design had escaped the drawing office.

Lodgings were intriguing and comparatively brief at first. Ted, my aeroplane friend and I were billeted on a family, father, who worked at the local American Air Force base, mother, older daughter who spent her evenings ensconced in the "front room" with her soldier boyfriend and the door shut and much prettier younger daughter who worked at Woolworths. The entire family resented us and eventually we were cast out. They didn't like "grammar school boys".

Probably the most intriguing machine in the works was the centreless grinder. This was devoted largely to finishing wing attachment bolts to the required accuracy of one ten thousandth of an inch. The unfinished bolts were presented to the girl operators a few thousandths of an inch oversize. The girls measured them, popped them in the grinder, counted a number of seconds related to their measurement, and removed them, accurate to one ten thousandth of an inch. This was due to the minute flexibility of the massive grinding machine.

I got myself billeted in company with the local personnel manager, on an older pleasant couple who were kindness itself, the lady was almost totally deaf and had a deaf aid which needed a motor cycle battery to power it, worn at the waist, the assembly being almost totally ineffective. She used to give me a package of sandwiches to take on the train journey home on Friday nights.

My fellow lodger brandished a 350cc, 1939 Matchless motor bike, which I envied, during the week and a wife and car at the weekend, when they vanished. It's probably unkind to say so but I cannot think of Newbury without feeling cold and wet.

Tom Barby was the overall manager of Shaw Works, a tall substantial figure wearing a light linen jacket (unheard of) in the summer, given to standing and surveying his domain from a conspicuous position on the shop floor.

One day a rogue apprentice suggested to one of his colleagues that he approach this figure and ask him to sell him an ice cream. He must have been a fool because he actually did it! Tom Barby was up to it. He just said "Run along sonny" and grinned. A happy unfortunately placed workshop.

My six months here was soon up and I looked forward to moving back to Southampton. Not a chance, I was transferred to South Marston, a large airfield and factory three miles north of Swindon. Antiquarians will note that the name means Pigs Hill, I meanly considered it appropriate.

South Marston was a very large factory built for Phillips & Powis makers of wartime trainers and taken over by Vickers just as a useful manufacturing facility. Presumably I was to be trained to do useful manufacturing. BAH. Little better than nothing, my first job was fitting the fairing to the underside of the rear gun turret of Wellington bombers which were being refurbished for Coastal Command. One fellow was installing gyros for the autopilot. They had been refurbished and he could with some difficulty carry them across the shop, they were heavy! I am constantly amazed that the two in my model aeroplane now weigh less than one gramme total.

About this time Pinewood film studios were making the film "Sound Barrier" and since it was about current jets Supermarine was on call to help, so the two organisations got acquainted. Pinewood mentioned that the studio needed all kinds of specialised equipment, and Supermarine, which had just stopped making five thousand aeroplanes a year and needing any work they could get, offered to step in.

Not being a movie man I cannot remember the names of the pieces of equipment we built, mostly mobile platforms of various kinds capable of placing men, lights, cameras, and even actors or groups of actors in positions and at heights suitable for the subject being filmed. One particular platform had a base consisting of deep fabricated girders. These were made from welded 2" angle iron, hundreds of pieces for many girders and it fell to me to cut these pieces with a hacksaw. I looked carefully at the job and concluded after a few cuts that I had neither the strength or the longevity to complete it, bonus or not.

I could arrive at this conclusion because, in the interest of education I had patrolled the entire plant to see what was what. I found in a distant region powered hacksaws and hydraulic shears which correctly applied could obviate all the heavy labour.

So I appropriated a "loose" four wheel trolley, loaded it up and moved the job to this strange shop, hoping nobody would notice.

I "smoked" the job, not without incident. On the second day I was called in to Joe Colvins office and accused of leaving the hydraulic driver on over the lunch hour, as reported by the foreman of the shop I was "pirating", who was himself present. I blushed (I hope) and pleaded guilty, expecting doom which I suppose showed in my demeanour.. To my surprise they both laughed (they had been leading me on). I was dismissed with the news that the time to do the job by hand would be retained so that my bonus would be gigantic. This money was spent on the purchase of a model plane engine, a Mills 2cc diesel engine. (I wonder what happened to it, it only flew twice & was a pig to start.) So I enjoyed that shop and eventually moved across the field to a truly wonderful shop.

This hanger was a multi purpose job. Near the door, was a very large space which was a final assembly and runup shop producing Spitfire Mk.24s and Seafire 47s, nearly identical but the Seafire had arrester gear and some had power folding wings. Occasionally VERY noisy runups. In the back of the hanger was a line of fuselage assembly jigs which started empty and finished full of fuselages ready for tail, wings, engine etc. It was my good fortune to, with a skilled "mate", fill a jig until the fuselage could be moved to the next stage. This was in the days of "direction of labour" so my skilled mentor was also a resentful professional footballer. He showed his resentment by taking a half hour break behind the hanger in the afternoons for a smoke. Otherwise all was smooth and very satisfying.

South Marston was the first of my moves that had anything other than work associated with it. I was billeted in a very large National Service Hostel, a very active wartime relic, at least 300 residents in separate minimal rooms, coming from all kinds of jobs and backgrounds, It had a large canteen supplying breakfast and evening meal, A dance floor, table tennis and other useful things. There were ladies and mens blocks confused only once during my stay. With the expected consequences!! My block was congenial, Ginger Colvin of my firm and Alan, apprentice of the Great Western Railway formed the local group, with other compatible characters scattered around the large site including fellow Supermarine apprentices.

There were two ways to get from Southampton to Swindon. You could travel by three successive buses or exceptionally slow train. Ginger Colvin got on the train one station before me and on one occasion chose his seat carefully in a compartment of girls, with whom he started a conversation inevitably. They turned out to be the chorus of the show appearing at the Empire, Swindon next week. Ginger leaned out of the window at my stop and dragged me in, he had already set up conversation.

It is not true about chorus girls, as was readily and pleasantly evident. They invited us to their show with free tickets and we went paying once each week. We went into town several times weekly to escort them home and if we were lucky we caught the last bus back to the hostel, or walked the three miles at 11pm. Diane Curtis came from Poole so we got along fine. Very nice all round and we met them again at Christmas in the pantomime. They all came to a dance at the Hostel which didn't do any of us apprentices much good since our combined dancing skill was virtually nil.

Our friend, Martin Harris worked about ten miles away and had to get up earlier than Supermariners so he was inveigled into being the Supermarine morning wake up person. I was a bit slow one morning and so he threw a knife at me through the window, fortunately it was a dinner knife.

Ginger and I lived in the same block as Alan, a railway apprentice. He was engaged to his foreman's daughter! (imagine). The family was based in Wales and Alan and his fiancee went there to visit. One morning he took his fiancee's breakfast up to her in bed. I have rarely seen a fellow so upset at the consequence. We had met the girl, she was very nice and Alan was frantic to marry her on $5 per week! He did.

Cycling back to the hostel in the dark adventures:- Met Ginger Colvins dad (my foreman) in the parking lot, his car wouldn't start. It was flooded. I told him to floor the accelerator and try. It went first go, my stock rose further. And on the way home a policeman noticed my bicycle rear light had been stolen, ten shilling fine. I had to borrow it from Ginger and pay back over five weeks.

While in Swindon I got a further academic setback. The company did not arrange for our continuation course in Southampton, so we had to go to Swindon Tech. This was unfortunate as that establishment did not give aeronautical courses and I was enchanted at taking a fascinating course in "Heat engines" Useless but I excelled, now two years behind normal. There was a time when I could prove that a car's thermal efficiency was directly proportional to its compression ratio. (It's terrible anyway but car people wont admit it.)

Half way through my time in Swindon my colleague told me that the union rate for a post apprentice draughtsman, aged 21, was five pounds eighteen shillings per week, a sum beyond the dreams of avarice, so I decided immediately to adopt this as my aim in life. Without my saying anything, slightly before I was 21, I was appointed to the drawing office, an inconceivable piece of good fortune! It was at it's wartime location in Hursley Park.

This was the former abode of Sir George Cooper who had acquired it by the assiduous production of beer and had surrendered it to become the design and experimental establishment of Supermarine when the original was bombed.

It consisted of large three story house, basement kitchens, stables and outbuildings, extensive grounds with deer, and a very large experimental hangar completely hidden by trees not to mention drawing offices, equally invisible from the air.

Also I had met a girl in the youth club. This one eventually decided to participate in this story on a permanent basis I am pleased to say. My arrival at home was fortuitous.

This young lady, Rosemary, worked for a solicitor in Southampton, typical old fashioned organisation with appropriate scales of pay. Learning of this I suggested she apply to Supermarine for a job which she did, succeeding admirably, nearly double the pay. I think her parents became less suspicious. They had some real reason to doubt the situation because when her mother tried to buy me a school scarf, she was told I was not on the school list. I also had two younger brothers at the school on their merits!! That will never be forgiven. She started work in the contracts department, later was transferred to the drawing office where a warning was issued (in view of my presence), NO SHENANIGENS.

New apprentice arrivals immediately went to work for Ron Vare (nobody called him Ron). The juveniles were lined up at their drawing boards in the office with Mr. Vare at their backs.

Our function was to get from him notes of anomalies in the drawings arriving from the widespread workshops. We had to investigate the situation and clear the drawings for reissue after his approval. Being youthful we did not always perform this function with due diligence. If you departed from your duty for a word with a fellow wage slave, Ron Vare was reputed to be able to burn holes in your back with his eyes. However in any tricky situation he always supported his lads.

I had after this a short useless session on the Seagull amphibian, successor to the much produced Walrus, both killed very quickly by helicopters, which as everyone knows, do not fly but are repelled by the earth because of their sheer ugliness.

I was surprised in due course to be transferred to Mr. Pelham G. Slades section, the ultimate definer of the largest component of the airframe. One job I remember clearly was to arrange ingress to the cockpit of the Swift. The aircraft could get to twenty five thousand feet altitude in a minute or so but you could easily spend a few minutes waiting for the other crews to finish with the steps. I did arrester hook attachments on the Scimitar, twin engine naval job which was actually built in small quantities and once took off from a carrier with its brakes locked! What are wheels for? I did a mainspar frame for that aircraft, not my proudest job but big, heavy and interesting. There are not many three quarter inch bolts in any aeroplane, and I also did boring fuselage skin plans. More skin than Supermarine was used to.

The first "Swift" was an Attacker fitted with swept wings and minus the 400 lb. of nose ballast. This did little more than prove you could fiddle about with an aircraft and with luck it could be better. The plane was brought nearer practicality by changing to tricycle undercarriage and variable incidence tailplane. This was done by an ad hoc modification of both ends of the fuselage. The nose was done by Slades section and the rear end by "Soapy" Hudson leading a subcontracted team. There was more than a little confusion here since the new nose was designed to be grafted on to one prototype and the rear end to another. The front was done as a legitimate add on to prototype VV 119 which was kept busy on flight trials until the rear end was ready. One day the aircraft was stripped of its wings, brought into Chilbolton flight shed and put in a jig. After careful perusal of the relevant drawings I was sent to Chilbolton with a red pencil and drew a red line round the rear fuselage, irregular in shape. Next day I came back and the fuselage aft of my red line was cut off and was gone. The new slightly different rear end, with the variable incidence tailplane was in the jig ready for a graft job. Its lines did not match VV119 but I had to produce a fair blend which, entirely fortuitously matched the current "area rule" requirement. One of the test pilots, Dave Morgan, walked by and said, jokingly I hope:-"Is that all that holds it together."

A very important change was the decision to use the ROLLS ROYCE AVON engine as opposed to the Attacker's usual Nene. This engine was of considerably smaller diameter than the Nene and I suppose the use of the Nene type fuselage was in the interest of speed of production, although it did not ultimately matter. The Russians were in no hurry! It was very odd to have all that space in a fighter aircraft.

Vickers at Weybridge were developing the Valiant four engine bomber and on one test flight a crack developed in the combustion section of one of its Avon engines from which a jet of flame virtually melted the wing structure and resulted in a total loss of the plane and crew.

It was decided to fit an ad hoc stainless steel liner to the Swift engine bay and I was given the job to extemporise, to be followed by a draftsman for the record.

Eric Cooper, assistant chief designer, was present at the critical lowering of the engine into place and obviously it was important to see that the guesswork steel didn't obstruct the engine from its correct installed position, which would have involved more complex stainless work. Everybody was peering from the top down the sides and could not see underneath. He said the best place to observe the fit was from where the jet pipe goes. Somebody said "Creedon's already there." Must have done me some good.

There was always something interesting going on. One time a hydraulic test pump got in to resonance with the aileron control. The noise was shocking as every tool and loose part was shaken to the floor and the deep interior of the aircraft. Nothing loose is mandatory in an aircraft and it took an hour to be sure there was nothing loose.

There were interesting characters running the experimental hanger, Tojo, the manager, so called because of an oriental appearance, Ted Stamps, inclined to throw things if crossed and Paddy Horne who could tie a one inch pipe in a knot on a personal diet of some kind of medicine.

This was before the invention of Philips head screws and power screwdrivers. As a result there was a definite problem on the Scimitar. The two engines were side by side and the engine covers extended over the entire top of the fuselage, and since they constituted a major part of the structure they required many 3/8" screws to hold them. Many in fact was about one hundred! The plane would have spent more time being unscrewed than fighting!

I put it about that a high speed fastener would be a good idea. P.G. Slade my benign section leader got permission from the deities for me to design one. I did, it was made and duly patented, worked like a dream. Self locking, two turns to close/open, full 3/8" strength, patented. Nobody wanted it, power screwdrivers were in the offing. A notebook of non specific work was kept in the office, my name and device were entered, as was the name of R.J. Mitchell previously. I expect the book was thrown away at the dissolution.

Hence I was delivered to the project office, fount of all knowledge and told to do something useful on a new aircraft, type 559. They needed a minion to do the menial tasks on this unusual configuration. It was a canard machine, tail first like the Wright Bros., Mach No. 2.4, all wet refrigerated (with fuel) wing, two jet engines one above the other and two small rocket engines of gigantic thrust. My only small contribution was to note that the carefully optimised positions of the foreplane spar and the nosewheel retraction pivot were about a foot apart. If you disturbed them slightly they could be combined, since they didn't work simultaneously, saving possibly 100lb. weight.

My usefulness there was soon exhausted and I was shunted back to Mr. Slade.

It was becoming increasingly clear that the long threatened move to South Marston was assuming the aspect of reality and that "something must be done"

Tom Turner, project office colleague, later vice president of Fairchild U.S.A had pirated his own highly detailed cutaway of the Swift to New York where "Aviation Week" (it was "Aviation" then) had offered him a job at $100 per week. He went on from there. The Pound sterling had recently dropped from $4.2 to the pound to $2.8, later $2.4 which made their wages fantastic. A strange thing was that several U.S. aircraft companys had discovered that a three line small ad in the Southampton paper would produce many replies, a large proportion were fruitful and we were losing a couple of people each week, in at least one case as an emergency measure to retrieve the companies pension plan money to pay off debts before vanishing across the Atlantic..

Also amongst the small ads. was an anonymous one asking for aircraft draughtsmen in the Southampton area. Unbelievable. We knew the local standbys, Follands and Saunders Roe were much the same as we were, facing trouble. Any way I applied. It turned out to be a branch of Sir Raymond Quilter's parachute company, set up by old pals of the Aeroplane Underground. I identified "Gillie" late of Cunliffe Owen, probable Cierva survivor Dan Cooper, the peripatetic H.C. Smith (one of two) and I firmly believe they were all in touch with each other by phone.

Anyway, by secret recommendation I landed on my feet there. It wasn't mentioned but they had contracted with Vickers Weybridge to do the dog work on the Viscount which was, worthily a hot number, about 300 sold in the U.S. alone. Weybridge also had the BAC111, the Vanguard and two four engine jobs going at the same time. It was rumoured that they were carpeting the hangers to use up the money. Strings of similar fuselage frames and the like was our expected diet.

It was called the G.Q. Parachute Company. H.C. Smith was D O head, "Bunny" Labett, an old school mate of mine was stress entirety, Ken Whitmarsh another school buddy was present on account of his shop & manufacturing skills. (He was also second best cyclist in Britain) and I did the aeroplane dogwork assisted by others of varying usefulness. Denis Prior was the fastest draughtsman on earth. It was pretty obvious they had been chosen. I could not have chosen a better team from Supermarine in spite of their quirky little ways. Good men, strong characters.

The work, as might be expected in a subcontract shop was fairly run-of the-mill. There was a slight altercation when we did a slipper fuel tank for the wing of the Viscount and Vickers omitted to tell us the dihedral angle. Hurried erasures! One good job was a wing structural test rig although none of us were conversant with the structural steel needed. The best job we did for Weybridge was the airstairs for the Vanguard, successor to the Viscount which had sold over 300 in the U.S. These stairs, designed to give access to the cabin without ground equipment, folded up mechanically into nearly zero space just inside the cabin entry door. I have to say that the Viscount airstairs folding geometry was one of the cleverest I have ever seen, we had to do the same, only 30% higher! There was no point in trying to improve on the folding geometry for the Vanguard. I took it and enlarged it by the necessary 30%. However, we had been preceded by a geometric genius but his stress analysis was probably non existent. I had to start from scratch. Just incidentally I got into an argument with Henry Smith as to whether you could resolve moments applied to a point as you can direct loads. I won. The work was straightforward but surprisingly laborious, it was rather surprising that the weight turned out to be 30% less for 30% larger job. Like all job shops, when they did not need us we were dropped instantly, the blow in this case being mysteriously softened by the workings of the old pals act.

I got a job at Saunders Roe back at Eastleigh Airport (ex Cierva}. It was superficially just fine, but the aeroplane underground had oversold me to the chief draughtsman and he had passed this view on to various people who like every aircraft man in the area were a bit worried about continued employment, particularly if they were older. There was always an underlying resentment that I had been employed in a "tight" market. I had the privilege of watching one of their Skeeter helicopters wreck itself when the engine refused to fire up on a practice autorotative descent. Shaken crew, tail cut off, tot of whiskey on the firm.

The Aeroplane Underground at that time was widespread. I had a Supermarine colleague, Ron Sherrin, working in Winchester at a company called Riley & Neate and he was aware that his boss Eddie Lee was seriously short on people to do the Gloucester Substation foundations. This is one of the places where switching of major electrical current round the country as required is done. He was also aware of the tacky doings of Saunders Roe (no reflection on the chief draughtsman). Don Dommet, another Supermarine Mafioso, had superbly enhanced our collective reputations by demonstrating a method of determining the minimum distance between three randomly directed straight lines, very useful if you had to position the downleads from a tower at 132,000 volts... avoids sparks or explosions. A true drafting masterpiece. I joined and did most of the

Gloucester foundations and in the process learned a little about reinforced and prestressed concrete work.

Any of the readers of this who have worked in the personnel department of a large company will, I am sure, realise that by now my resume was shockingly fractured, and probably think because of this that they had better steer clear of me. I never encountered this myself since I suppose that the number of fractured resumes caused by the war must have been pretty large and I think latterly the commendation of people who knew me did some good.

A large part of my attention was always on staying employed, not necessarily easy with 50% of my type of job evaporated from the area, but I did have an actual life. Thinking back a few pages you may recall the girl I met at the youth club. She was very well organised but eventually got to see that we might have possibilities, so we got married. While I was at Riley & Neates our daughter was born, everything correct and pretty neat. Our tracer and tech. girls in the office were delighted in addition to all the usual aunts, uncles and new grandparents.

A member of the staff was Bill Kyte, youthful engineer and contemporary of Peter Selwood, scion of

SELWOOD FOR PLANT which sign was generally scattered at least around Hampshire and Bristol. Peter had a degree in engineering from London University. Bill mentioned to me that Peter was investigating on his fathers behalf inertial flow in pipes because, being in the plant hire business he rented out an old fashioned diaphragm pump which on occasion delivered twice its calculated output.

He also had the mandate to improve the depth and reliability of the suction performance of their pump. "Why wouldn't it suck up the 30 ft. odd which the atmosphere promised?" Well, Peter and I got in to this in as much depth as was warranted. I suppose we must have engaged in general chat along these and other lines for some months and in conjunction with the themes of inertia and suction came up with a gadget that combined both. Peter turned up with a five pound pot of mercury, the expense of which made us feel bound to do something or indeed practically anything. This enabled us to do impossible water experiments indoors at one thirtieth of the water experiments size.

We came up with a 40" copper pipe with a rubber sleeve and a one way valve, in only, at one end and a piston and spout at the other end, all of which we filled with the mercury.

Whether you follow this or not when you banged the piston down the bottom rubber sleeve swelled, contracted and threw the entire mercury column up and some came out of the spout 40" higher while the column was kept full by the one way in valve at the bottom. Thus we had 40" nominally impossible lift combined with inertial flow.

"Father", as W.R. Selwood was known throughout the organisation decided that it would be a good idea if these simple insights could be developed. He also felt that the earthmover hydraulics were being uneconomically dealt with in his company. This was a large and expensive area of their operations. Characteristically he figured that if I were running a hydraulic maintenance shop I would be around to talk to Peter, two birds with one stone as always. So once again I changed jobs this time to one that was visibly prosperous, hope springs eternal!

After a few months I got a hydraulic test rig built and in profitable operation with the help of a very good assistant and was free to chat about our other insights. We decided that if we ran our pump faster we

71

could both make it smaller and improve the inertial part of the flow. The problem was that ordinary circular motion, when driven at our ambitious speed produced literally smashing accelerations, which of course was why our projected device did not already exist. So our initial decision was to drive the piston with a cam which would control the almighty bang and convert it into a respectable shove. We soon dropped this. Imagine a beautiful polished, shaped cam doing one thousand revolutions per minute in an atmosphere of dirty sandy water! Sealed roller bearings eventually did the job.

So a thousand times a minute we had to store the excess of high pressure water available. We fitted the cylinder head with a rubber sleeve stretched over a perforated sealed tube which just swelled up a bit when the bump came and normally rested against the perforated tube. This combination of crank and cushion eventually turned out very well and we got a water flow through our inertial tube of about two and a bit times the displacement of the cylinder. To handle priming the pump, since air has little inertia, we had simple flap valves.

There were lots of stages in the development of these embodiments. Firstly we worked only with one cylinder and the piston, because of the very short stroke was and still is connected rigidly to the connecting rod. The sealing of the piston was achieved after much experiment by, inevitably, a toroidal ring of rubber, the rubber toroid having molded in attachment to the piston and the cylinder wall and a high measure of precompression to prevent fatigue. This seal, the hardware heart of the machine would run for one thousand hours at fifty P.S.I. external load, proven the hard way which is a tale in itself. We ran thousand hour proving tests when we had...not without great exertion, got everything O.K. A thousand hours is about six weeks, night & day If it broke down in that time it was as well to start again as soon as possible.

This of course led to frequent monitoring, me on the 11p.m. run. One night I found the place on fire...! I ran across the road to the phone box but I had no change! However 999 calls do not need money so I got the fire service. Mrs Haskell, of whom later, had already done so. Then I tried to call "Father" without money. Fire or not, no money, no call. The fire brigade arrived and I had to tell them that near the seat of the fire were some welding cylinders. To show them, I had to move towards the cylinders. I did this VERY hesitantly. The firemen didn't do this. They CHARGED smashing windows as they went, cold water was on those cylinders in seconds. I was told later that those cylinders would not be used because of their experience.

Mrs. Haskell occupied a site next to Selwood and ran a thriving ballast and gravel business which apparently needed a 50ft. tower like structure for its operation. One day a large truck mounted portable crane turned up and started to place a box like structure on the top of this tower, about a 10ft. square space. The driver was having some difficulty, he was on his own and had nobody "up top" to guide things along. The truck had stabilizer legs extending about 4 feet either side. The ground was soft. I watched him for a while, he made few movements and I looked away. The ground literally shook and when I looked back the crane, truck and payload were flat on their sides, the soft earth was not good enough. The truck surprisingly had the gearbox snapped off the engine. Enlivened the dull moment! Nobody was hurt.

"Father" was a strange mixture. He used to dish out Christmas bonus's, but he did not pay well. When he heard that our street was to receive its first permanent surfacing, sidewalk, drainage etc. at a cost of about one quarter of my years salary, my Christmas bonus matched the number. On another matter he was always a bit inclined to dismiss his most expensive employees and promote their deputy, of course at a lower salary, but extra enthusiasm. His company had been built by him and two partners, when his then boss in London had sent him to Southampton to see if the blitz had made a construction equipment company there a good idea. It was, he didn't tell his boss. His first sale was a second hand steam roller, followed by getting the agency for a small cement mixer and dump truck. Both were ideal for all the local ambitious small builders within a thirty mile radius of a blitzed town. By the time I knew him the company was worth five million pounds (1976). Buzz Hibberd was one director, he accused me of continually walking past his office window so I would be noticed. He was wartime R.A.F. and flew anti submarine Catalinas in the war. He wanted to know why I didn't wear a suit to work. On one company occasion my wife told him with suitable emphasis. He was apparently under the impression that thinking precluded working.

Peter Selwood had a younger brother, Tim who was slightly disabled, having had polio some years before. Father was justifiably sensitive on the subject and when an N.H.S. service vehicle appeared at the gate offering free polio vaccinations father dictated that if you wanted to continue working for him you had better get done, (and good for him.) I had the pleasure, admittedly hard earned of saying no. I had to explain that due to my families experience I had been vaccinated three years before, priority from my brothers polio bout.

We got all our pump tests done, full load 1000 hours, dry run 24 hours and lowest possible capacity, all of which were done with sandy water and to the relief of Buzz Hibberd, who thought the whole thing was a waste of money. A sales launch date was set.

Father Selwood was in his element. He managed to get most of our companies equipment involved in the pump demo. Cranes held a delivery hose 60ft. in the air, deep and dirty holes were dug with just a trickle of water in them (the most difficult pumping job), pumps were dragged through mud behind dump trucks and great gushers were organised. The rope holding the delivery hose, gushing 60 feet in the air broke. Someone asked, "Who tied that hose up there?" Buzz Hibberd's reply was "Someone who used to work here"... the image he liked to project. The whole thing was very well organised. Father must have got at least fifty companies representatives, possible buyers there that day.

Buzz Hibberd, never a believer, said we would sell 30 by Christmas and 200 next year (it was September). We sold 30 that day and 200 by Christmas!

However this was the happy ending of major effort. Father decided, and said so. It was not his intention to continue any design-development work. So he said to me that I had a job there as long as I wanted it but it would be something different. Didn't really suit me.

So I was off to a new and surprising branch of the underground, My next door neighbour of all people.

Peter Gilbert had joined Pirelli from school, worked in Eastleigh all his life, knew everything., and was pretty sharp. He knew what was going on and thought I might fit. So I did.

About 1850 an engineer called Vignoles had cut three mile tunnel through the Pennines, England's spinal mountain chain to allow the not too hot locomotives of the day to cross the country. A hundred years later the original tunnel was becoming decrepit, the cheapest thing to do was to cut another alongside it. This left a somewhat decrepit tunnel entirely suitable for sufficient refurbishment for non rough usage. Accordingly the Central Electricity Generating Board who had a dreadful time trying to run simple overhead lines across any picturesque landscape, especially mountains, were forced to consider underground cable, and the "under" was freely available.

Do not think that they could just pop the same wires through the tunnel, the cables were insulated, water cooled and had snake like curves to allow thermal changes of length, They also had to be firmly tied down because if one went bad the others would be violently magnetically displaced. As a first estimate the cost is always about ten times that of an overhead tower line.

The cable is about 5" in diameter and starting at the outside there is about a quarter inch of PVC to protect against the world, very thin copper to keep the TV out, lead, to keep the coolant in, about an inch or so of paper soaked in oil to keep the electricity in, two square inches of copper to do the actual work, and to be sure there is no nasty ionised air about a central half inch oil duct. Quite a lot compared to a simple overhead cable. In the three mile tunnel two concrete channels were needed for immersion of the six warm cables in water which had to be kept flowing. To design the installation machinery we had to measure the stiffness of the cable. It was about the same as a 1-1/4" iron bar! (but not as springy.) In addition it weighed about 100 lb. per yard. The whole length of the job was three miles Six of these monster cables had to be set in neat slightly snaked (about 2") paths and clamped down in two concrete troughs. In anticipation of this task a narrow gauge railway ran throughout the length of the tunnel with a neat electric locomotive.

This loco. towed a simple string of T shaped trolleys, each with two wheels, which carried three cables one above the other, slightly wavy in the vertical plane to match the final installed horizontal 2" wave (matching lengths were critical.)

With train standing still, the temporarily disconnected locomotive pulled a zip fastener like device past the train which was locked in position, so that it lifted the cable continuously off the train and transferred it sideways to its correct position over the side of trough where it drooped slowly to its design position in the trough. The zip fastener was notable. It had to hold up about 600 lb. of cable, bend it up to 8ft. sideways and was adjustable to put it down accurately to the half inch.

I found out much later that nobody really believed a word of this and they took a piece of scrap cable (of which more later) and constructed a significant sample length and tried it out. Perhaps wisely, but it did work and not only on paper.

It is noteworthy that each joint at 100 yard intervals, on each one of these cables, took three men working 24 hours with no break to complete, and there was a total of 18 miles.

The scrap cable used in the trial had an interesting origin. It started life as a totally normal useable cable. Now to get cable into the Fawley tunnel under Southampton Water, which was another very good job which Pirelli made a successful bid on, it was necessary to get it down the 150 ft. vertical entry shaft. Fifty yards at 100lb. per yard is a good weight. It was arranged to have a continuous loop of adequate rope run from top to bottom of the shaft and lash the descending portion of the cable to the rope which was slowly cycled so that the lashings could be made and unmade at the top and bottom respectively. How many lashings do you need in 150 ft.? This was subject to experiment, the less lashings the quicker you could get the cable down. They approached the limiting case and got the whole lot down in one WHOOSH. Nobody was hurt. After that they had a spare piece of cable.

They also wanted a "damn sure" brake on the system, so this time they thought they had better get some advice. The brake was easy but what was to hold the brake? A quarter, half or perhaps the whole lot might might be bucketing down the shaft at 20 or 30 ft. per second. Well they stop big trucks on dangerous slopes with gravel, so with my microscopic knowledge of soil mechanics I checked the local gravel and told them to dig a long trench and anchor a specific size of steel plate in it and tie it to the brake. It was in fact a gravel parachute. Winning is not possible. They looked at my measly gravel and decided this would not hold it. (True of course-don't lock your brakes). So they threw out my carefully designed braking material and filled the trench with GOOD SOLID WELL PACKED EARTH. Fortunately the brake was not needed. I still wonder how that man got his job.

A man called Christopher Cockerel at that time had demonstrated lifting and moving considerable weights by feeding a cushion of air under them. The disadvantages of this are by no means as obvious as the advantages. If you double the size of the vehicle it needs twice the power to run the confining edge jets, however doubling the power gives four times the area/lift hence payload. Christopher Cockerell had got government funding to see if anything usefull could be extracted from what superficially at least looked very promising. He had set up an establishment on Southampton Water to research this and had attracted a worthy technical staff.

Now at that time the American government was trying to influence the government of Vietnam and there was somewhat violent controversy going on there which included mining the countries waterways, an important mobility asset. So if you could travel over the water rather than through it you might well avoid the mines. Accordingly Bell Aerosystems of Buffalo N.Y. were contracted to look in to this, which they did by a small ad. in the Southampton newspaper, resulting in an almost total flow of the British hovercraft staff to Buffalo N.Y., including my brother... who provided me with much useful information. I was financially stable, but the only progress I was making was on the basis of house appreciation, which has a negligible effect on your life. I checked my brothers salary and concluded that I could, on the basis of my American potential, kill my mortgage in two years and come home free.

I wrote to my model aeroplane friend, Ted Clarke who had jumped ship to the U.S. years before to ask him what he thought.. He had always lacked financial conservatism, bought a motor bike on three pounds a week, so he said I would be lucky to save six hundred dollars in my two year scheme, certainly not the five thousand I was looking for. So I ignored him. My brother was there, living a life of reckless abandon, he provided much financial planning advice, housing, cars, food, the constituents of cost of living, high or low.

So I wrote to Bell, got an offer, chatted them up an extra ten dollars a week, and started the somewhat daunting process, more difficult than most because of the fixed objective.

We were required to go to the American Embassy in London, all four of us, presumably to see if we were real. We had a medical (each) and an interesting interview during which I was advised that I was within the range of the draft (for Vietnam). Travelling we had a mattress in the back of the car since with an early start it was a fifteen hour day with two small children. William fell asleep. When he woke up he asked: "Which day did we get up."

We had the choice of air or sea travel, sea made you look more steady, at least in those days and it would be our only vacation that year. Anyway I had watched the Queen Mary for years from my bedroom window it was "our" ship.

We could not afford to leave the house empty for two years so set about renting it. It went to a Dutch employee of I.B.M. pretty safe and covered the mortgage. Our bank manager thought we should sell it but I said we could never afford to buy it back because of housing inflation My guess of its value after two years was only 200 pounds or 3.3% wrong.

Somewhat to our surprise we found that this was the last Westbound service crossing Queen Mary would make, which mandated the purchase of the commemorative goblet. From subsequent experience we found that passenger transport was not in the least like cruise ship travel. The crew were a bit downhearted, the class thing was a little obvious and children, with us were hidden in a corner at mealtimes. The absence of the nanny was fairly obvious. It was clear that traditionally only the wealthy crossed the Atlantic. Anyway the dancing was good, the band liked us and if you synchronized your dancing with the roll of the ship it was an unusual experience, all downhill. WE WERE HANDED OUR GREEN CARDS AS WE GOT OFF THE SHIP. It was obvious that Bell Aerosystems had an excellent path through immigration bureaucracy.

We made our way through pouring rain to La Guardia, ate a hot dog, my first American food, and eventually, to our gratified surprise, boarded a BAC 111 (British} for Buffalo. We mentioned the rain, there was a storm right across the state, and we got my bumpiest ride ever. William, youngest was sick, Helena next was not quite sick and we felt decidedly queasy. When we got out of the plane there was literally the heaviest rain I had ever seen. One of our predecessors wives had taken on the job of settler and efficiently drove us to my brothers house where we had chance to take a deep breath. Mick, Joyce and Sarah rented a four bedroom house and we were able to stop and try to catch up. Our eventual objective was to rent our own accommodation at the lower, i.e. cheaper level of respectability. Due to their generosity we were able to get a good two year base set up.

Presumably on the basis of my having spent a couple of years dealing with large amounts of fluid the group I was thrust upon was the rocket test mob, we had to arrange test rigs. The section was probably left over from the Bell X 1, the rocket propelled, first ever supersonic aircraft. These rockets were a bit more evil, probably part of an ICBM that sent its multiple warheads to different destinations. A good idea if you thought the Russians were about to attack but for the most part incredibly boring. The section was known as the post boost propulsion system. I was placed next to Jim M., a slightly black fellow who stopped me making a complete idiot of myself with a bit of gentle, necessary introductory guidance. He used to amuse me by telling of drive by shootings on his street. Ed Seymour my section leader was helpful and aware that whatever our abilities, we were "fish out of water". We were busy at our newly rented accommodation on Nassau Avenue. I built bunk beds for the children and was astounded no less by the superb quality and low price of the timber I needed. Its no wonder they don't build many timber houses in England.. We were introduced also to double glazing, not to mention a few weeks later, to the reason for it. The rent was (by design) low for Buffalo, we had to get our mortgage target. Our neighbours were very welcoming, they were nice people. Helena, our daughter made friends with Phyllis across the street and an old couple used to chat at length with three year old William, turning him in to a partial American. It is the unfortunate truth that at first their welcome was a result of our not being coloured, genuine nonetheless. So much for cheap rent. We bought on HP a 1964 Chevrolet Bel Air, all part of the cast iron budget.

Bell Aerosystems had a standard way of settling in new English arrivals of whom they had quite a few, but we were less expensive because my brother and Joyce took practically the whole burden, no motel, no meals out, so the lady in charge, the English wife of one of the hovercraft mob, took us all seven to a nice dinner of unBritish proportions. So I toiled for a while preparing drawings of assemblies of proprietory parts selected by an "engineer" as instructed by the person who designed the rocket. It is unkind and only slightly true to add "if any". They were small, certainly no more than one thousand pounds thrust.

We were absolutely astonished at Christmas by the way individual houses were decorated, some of them had hundreds of coloured lights. Totally unBritish exuberance and very uplifting. You thought you might actually get to like this place which had hitherto been a bit what the Germans call "unheimlich". Nice people but crazy.

I had one adventure that, although I didn't realize it at the time, was responsible for our success in this oversize foreign venture.

Some rockets are a bit touchy about where they are pointing when lit up, too little or too much fuel can make fires or loud bangs, so the test guys decide on something perceived nasty and light it up to make sure it is acceptable. My test was 30 degrees tail down so in order to prevent the blast digging a hole in the concrete or worse, the test rig had to be ten feet up in the air. Easy enough to arrange but the rocket, instead of trying to lift the test rig in the usual way, tries to push the whole rig over. If not given the appropriate attention you might have a rogue rocket skidding round the site or hitting buildings.

I saw my job as preventing the rig tipping over. I had a reasonable grip of overturning calculations and the foundations thereof leftover from my Gloucester substation days, so I just behaved normally and put in a foundation suitable to keep the rig from tipping over or skating, sled like into the building in which I happened to be working.

I finished it and took it to Ed Seymour, my section leader a thoroughly nice person who, I suspect was proud of having assistants recruited from abroad. He looked and after a short pause, presumably from astonishment said, "What's this?"...I was a little taken aback, I said we had to take the overturning force. He was a bit silent while I gave him an outline. Apparently for those guys the design world had always stopped under their feet. He recovered his equilibrium and we proceeded normally from there on. I formed the opinion that they had avoided previous disaster due to the diligence of their "pick and shovel" men who figured "stuff like that must be well dug in". Not by any means the first or only occasion in my experience when lack of cross disciplinary knowledge was dangerous or at the very least expensive. I don't think they had any significant overturning jobs before. Come review time I got a good raise, and Ed Seymour's boss acknowledged my presence when encountered.

Now Bell in their recruitment literature made it clear to us that they had, I think, more than 150 government contracts. True but half their value lay in just one of those....number 8533 the post boost propulsion system, the one 75% of our section was working on... they cancelled it!

Just to emphasize the problem, the prehistoric photocopying machine on which I and several others were busily copying (pirating) our resumes caught fire!

Calspan was a design group associated with the University of Buffalo, Tex Johnson, the pilot who rolled the first Boeing 707 during a public display, had somehow got a small design group there who were converting an elderly Convair 540 into a Concorde simulator, at low speed only of course. This involved fins fitted on the wings and an extended nose with second cockpit. This group, commanded by a chilly Scotsman, needed a couple of draftsmen. I applied and was turned down. Next day I got an offer from them at a small increase in pay. The underground in the form of Ed Seymour were at it again. Anyway I went there. Thankfully I may say. Nothing this bad had happened since Alf Hucknall got laid off in Toronto when the Canadians dropped the F86 Sabre. (He had been there two weeks) You may think this was enough of a diversion but I had scattered resumes to the four winds and most functionaries are slower than the immediate word of mouth typical of the aircraft mafia.

Carborundum of Niagara falls had developed a composite armor and were in the process of designing a shock attenuating armored seat for helicopters. They had virtually nobody to do the job except Bill C whose qualifications were a navy service friendship with the elite of Carborundum, considerable experience of flying over the Pacific in the single engine "Bent Wing Bird" of Consolidated Vultee together with the belief that anyone who could do that could do anything. It seems to me that as an extrovert sociable service type he was well qualified to purvey simple body armour to the military, which he did, almost like selling suits. However aircraft seat design is in a very different class which he fell into without the extensive technical and background resources needed. He got authority without an inkling of the tools needed.. He should have been dictatorial to his bosses and partner to his staff. As far as I was concerned only his ideas on pay were correct.

By this time after a few months at Carborundum, including a few Lear Jet trips, visits to customers and potentially interested service divisions, it was getting near to planning withdrawal to home base in England.

We had covered our mortgage, saved enough to return and set ourselves up again to find an English job.

We thought that while we were still here we might as well have a look around. So we borrowed a friends tent trailer, hitched it to the back of the Chevy and set out for the wild west equipped with our 35mm movie camera, (cost $35 new) bought when we first arrived. We saw what everyone wants to see, connected for the most part by endless freeway. We saw the Devils Tower and the Badlands, Laramie and real western steam trains which we raced and an eight mile stretch of embryonic freeway in Wyoming which we shared with massive earth movers. We saw Jackson Hole and its airport, a snake, Laramie, a John Wayne stagecoach and the Grand Tetons and Mount Rushmore. In Yellowstone a friendly bear got up and peered in our car window and we saw "Old Faithful" For Real!! And for the most part we fixed our own food, and slept in our trailer. We arranged for William to emerge from a saloon through batwing doors, and we eventually drove back to reality. Get Home.

First we had to get school starting dates, Williams first ever, and book flights to suit. I foolishly thought Prestwick-Eastleigh, much nearer home but the Prestwick wait proved me wrong! They did get home with the help of neighbour Francis. Then it was me. I intended staying til Thanksgiving so I first had to find accommodation since I didn't want to keep the house. I found a bed-sitter in Niagara Falls, convenient for work.

At about the worst possible time the transmission in the Chevy quit. Two speed, totally unfit for towing. I only just managed to break out of my deliberately induced micro management of money to get it repaired and I actually found someone to buy the car and take me to the airport in it on my chosen day. The flight left in the evening on Thanksgiving Day. You might be surprised at how difficult it is to get anything to eat other than a THANKSGIVING DINNER on that day. Macdonalds don't care! Another of the problems was that as always on the days leading up to Thanksgiving there are no available seats to any transatlantic airport or anywhere else for that matter.

On the evening of an exceedingly boring Thanksgiving day I flew in a nonedescript twin jet to Boston where eventually I boarded a VC10 built by Vickers, Weybridge. I was lucky to get this experience as the VC10 was not exactly flooding the market.

It demonstrated why when we stopped at Bangor, Maine to top up the fuel for the Atlantic crossing.

My arrival home was all one could wish for, including brilliant autumn sunshine when we went to fetch the children from school. Rosemary's father had been paying much attention to the house and things were all in good shape. All I had to do was get a job. There was a bit of a setback there since although my tunnel job at Pirellis had turned out well, they were waiting for a new contract with the Railway for overhead line installation, so I had to look round. There was a small company in Southampton called Archiprint Services, founded originally to provide local architects and any one else who needed it with a "print room" as required. No doubt as a result of their contacts they were fairly heavily into subcontract drafting with branches at Farnborough and in East Anglia where there had always been a flourishing subcontract field lead by Marshalls of Cambridge. I saw their small ad for draughtsmen and fixed up an interview. I should stop being surprised. The boss was my old colleague from the weight section at Supermarine, Ken Russel. The tentacles of the underground are everywhere, and moreover Ken had an appreciation of where I had stood at Supermarine so there was little hesitation in offering me the job he had, which was at Farnborough where he had a thriving sub contract business going. I had to have something to tide me over until Pirelli matured so in spite of the 40 mile commute I jumped at it. Some of my colleagues were interesting. One, who proved to be harmless was bad tempered beyond belief, another recorded in writing even the most trivial events around him but there was no trouble in the organisation. We had mostly unchallenging work from Farnborough with other bits and pieces from the Cambridge area where there was another branch of Archiprints.

We got in to an amusing controversy with Farnborough. We were told we had in our possession an exotic research antenna, from a prior contract (it was a coil of wire). We couldn't locate it and did not believe we still had it and said so. We got an irate response. Our record keeping freak heard about this and entirely spontaneously notified them of the time, date and method of return. I think there was still some of the job insecurity of the fifties and sixties about.

Our hot tempered friend got in late one morning looking slightly the worse for wear. He said nothing and we dare not ask. During the course of the day it slowly appeared that he had got into an altercation with another motorist on the way to work, resulting in a fight!

I had one small personal success which made me feel better. We were doing work for a company in East Anglia which was working on a "hovertrain," basically a train with no wheels but air cushions instead under the entire vehicle, obviously eliminating wheel friction. Since the track was necessarily prepared only to civil engineering standards, conventional suspension was thought to be needed and a torsion bar type was proposed. In the manner of most vehicles with this kind of suspension the torsion bars were proposed to be mounted across the vehicle.. Calculation showed that the vehicle was too narrow to allow a simple torsion bar to do the job and that parallel or concentric elements would be necessary, a rather inelegant-i.e. expensive configuration. My solution which was adopted was to place the torsion bars longitudinally, regaining most of the advantages at very little if any extra cost. Not intuitive. The reputation of Archiprint services was, I was told much enhanced. In fact they hinted I should be running it. But I would have to leave my hard earned house and go somewhere expensive.

Peter Selwood felt that my deal at his company was a bit raw. He showed this in a rather spectacular way. He bought a new(!) New Zealand made aeroplane and learned to fly it. He then said that if I could find an instructor I could learn on it at the cost of the petrol. My daughter, then about fifteen, had a friend whose father, in the R.A.F, had been a "Lightning" pilot accustomed to waving at Russian "Bear" pilots on patrol North of Scotland. Not every one has their daughter find them a flying instructor, for three pounds an hour he was prepared to instruct me! When I got back to Pirelli my colleagues had the daunting experience on occasion of watching me through the office windows on final approach to land. I sincerely hope they didn't see my first solo where I looked exactly like and was, a beginner landing in a 20 knot crosswind. The Airtourer is a remarkably forgiving aeroplane. My instructor had a good understanding of the role of fear in pilot training, he didn't even watch that landing. I did get my P.P.L.

Eventually after about six months I was actually welcomed back to Pirelli, where I was slowly introduced to the railway temperament, coupled with their defensive and adversarial feeling. I may have been oversold.

They had always installed their overhead power lines above the tracks by hand. I got the impression that to change any of their working mode for any reason, even proposed improvement, would involve possibilities that might not be understood, i.e. career threatening, expensive, needing thought, or dangerous. It was only people at the top who were foolish enough to propose innovation. There were working supervisors who knew the entire part numbering system of the present setup, a considerable investment. Their leaders were scarcely aware of this bias and it was a considerable and completely unnecessary burden to us. The section of railway we were to deal with ran from Euston to Crewe.

Most of our job involved six or four parallel tracks. To do the job the original way, for each headspan (the crosswires that held the whole lot up at 80 metre intervals), all tracks would have to be closed with radio communication with the signal system and the area would be flooded with men for perhaps a quarter hour, involving of course prolonged line closures.

What we had to do was design a device which, occupying only one side track, would enable the hanging of the across-track pre-assembled components (headspan) without impeding the other three or five tracks. Aside from the will to use it which was somewhat lacking it was a sensible notion.

The first thing to be done was to erect on the floor of a large shop the adjustable characteristics of every possible track cross section, so that in effect the two uprights either side of the track, any where along the track could be replicated flat on the floor. We could then build the appropriate supports for the longitudinal wires, the important current carrying ones, and finally take the headspan out and hang it from the already installed steel posts across the tracks, thus putting in position the correct support for the current carrying wires along the tracks they were intended for. The most successful tool was this floor, very simple to understand, it was just a great big adjustable picture of the entire job at stations anywhere along the sixty miles or so.

You could then actually build a long bundle of equipment for each location for our main rig to install.

This main rig was quite a complex device. It stood, when working, on the edge track at one side of the perhaps six track line and lifted the entire assembly across the five or six tracks, higher than the trains which had to pass underneath, to be hung on the prepared trackside masts. It looked rather like an ordinary tower crane The design difficulty of this machine lay in the fact that in spite of its twenty feet working height and the fact that it had to stretch across six tracks while stood on the edge one, it also had to travel in the normal running space to pass through tunnels and narrow cuttings, like a normal railway coach. We had a 60 ft. machine balancing on a 4'-8" base which had to take a mobile load of perhaps up to 1000lb. The counterweight design alone was extremely space constrained and at one time it was thought that sufficient weight of concrete could not be got into the available space. Anyway it went to work successfully and the gurus of the railway who had asked for the machine decided they could not give it sufficient time on site to be effective!

While we were waiting to send it to its work place at Crewe the Railway parked it 30 ft. high inline with the main runway approach at Eastleigh Airport!

There was a fear (only in the higher ranks of the railway) that the whole mass of the overhead wiring might, if correctly shaken at the right speed turn in to a giant trampoline. Fortunately I was not required to look in to that. However I did get consent to look in to a radical change where a powered pantograph followed a wire allowed almost to hang naturally, with little help at the supports. I got quite a long way with this (the work is still valid) when an almighty spanner flew in to the works.

I cycled home to lunch one day in my usual manner, to be greeted at the table by a much postmarked, bulging letter in obviously American format.

We did not open it for a while, we guessed its contents and were stunned. Carborundum wanted us back! On examination the conditions were a little strange, the salary wasn't however, and in view of the very modest progress we had made financially in the three years we had been at home we had to pay attention.

We should have paid much more attention to the recommended steps laid out. Firstly, we had to pay our own fares, to be refunded later. Secondly we were to stay with his secretary who would be pleased to accommodate us for a modest fee. Talk about a red flag which we didn't notice! In view of what it meant to us we pushed aside these somewhat odd stipulations, we had bigger concerns obviously. There was however the factor of immigration. We had "green cards" which allow you to leave the U.S. and re-enter after a short period. We had been gone for a long period and thought we could not just go back. We didn't know that a simple lie would suffice so we started the whole ghastly re-entry procedure from scratch. We could have rolled up at Niagara Falls and said we had been to Toronto for the day. It would have been in line with the general somewhat mendacious tone of the affair. We also sent most of our household goods by sea. The move took several months to arrange.

Before I had chance to really assess the situation we needed to get a house, staying with the bosses secretary was, it turned out, not the best arrangement, aside from the fact that Mr. was a gun man and there were powder trails running through the house.

We found a good house, reasonably priced, in Lewiston and bought it by what to us was strange, assumption of the previous owners mortgage (and his credit rating?) The banker who sold it to us was prepared to shake hands on the deal with me, but not Rosemary!

We began getting suspicious before we got a call from New York saying that if we didn't collect our furniture from the dock they would throw it in the water! That truly opened our eyes to the fact that we were in a bad situation. We were rescued by someone in the transport department at Carborundum who was a neighbour of our new house who fiddled it through. XXXXXXXXX

The "staff" I was presented with seemed to consist of a couple of recent high school graduates of doubtful talent and less industry.

In addition to the Sikorsky helicopter seat they now had a contract from Boeing for a much more sophisticated three dimensional attenuating seat. It must have been the old pals act because performance on the Sikorsky contract, or lack of it, was beginning to be apparent. It was beyond my masters capacity to appreciate that three dimensional work is more complex than two dimensional. He insisted that a basic geometry drawing was not needed! I tried very hard, some nights I did not get home til 2 a.m. and from the customers point of view I was the substantive contact.

Things were bad, I was isolated from my. bosses superiors who by nature were more akin to him than any engineering. They were simple grindstone makers who had stumbled on to knowledge that grindstones were very hard and with a little bit of fiberglass to help, could both smash and stop a wide variety of bullets.

I found out that my predecessor who had been poached from a local university had become so enraged that he left after an altercation without bothering with any further contact, leaving his due pay!

Moreover I now had a house to sell on two continents and had to find a job.

At that time there was a normal Middle East dust up which caused a lot of worry about oil supplies, speed limit of 55 m.p.h. and rationing threats (the proposed method of rationing was irrational and provided the only joke of the time). So nuclear affairs showed signs of life. About 30 miles south of Buffalo was a nuclear fuel reprocessing plant, very sensible idea, and it was decided that the mothballs should be removed in case it was needed. This was quite a job and fortunately they needed me. I couldn't get there fast enough but it was so far from Lewiston I had to stay near the plant four nights a week.

Under the illusion that this job looked pretty sound we sold (!) the Lewiston house and bought a lovely one in Hamburg (?) South of Buffalo. I was nicely settled when the oil crisis evaporated overnight and there was a mass ejection of staff. I'm not sure I was there a year but the underground was in full operation. Vic Barnhart, who was also ejected, with whom I had a good working relationship at the nuclear plant found a company in Pittsburg, very nuclear but a bit short on hardware, which needed some work on nuclear fuel transport, a subject with a poor public image. He was to do the nuclear shielding, about 20 tons of steel, and I was to do the carrying, which had to be designed on the basis that any part of it could fail but there should be no consequence.

Suited me, lots of fine aircraft are designed on this principle so I'm fully up to speed. So while I fished for a job I did this at home, very profitable and I could have gone to work for them! Pittsburg? Incidentally there were patents involved and it transpired that my fail safe method was patented by that companies entire technical staff as inventors, talk about safety in numbers.

Another fellow ejectee, Bill Tallboy had got a job at Union Carbide in Buffalo, and I achieved a truly bizarre employment offer with his help. I wrote to Union Carbide for a job and was turned down, I wrote to one of Union Carbide's suppliers and was turned down after an interview. But this supplier told Union Carbide he had had an application from a fellow he thought would be ideal for them. The Union Carbide people asked Bill Tallboy if he knew anyone who might be useful. He told them about me, they thus had two independent recommendations for a person they had already turned down, so I did join them. Personnel departments?

This was a real job with competent managers and it also happened to be interesting and intriguingly novel. Volkswagen had at last made a departure from the "Beetle" and were looking to Union Carbide, a specialist in heat exchangers, to do them an aluminium core radiator with plastic tanks.

The essential part of this radiator was many flat tubes each made of two very thin plates welded together. The plates were pressed before welding with bumps so that when the multiple finished tubes were stacked together there were gaps between them for air to flow through. The plates were only one hundredth of an inch thick. If a normal arc or gas welder were asked to do this weld his answer would be an emphatic no. The metal would heat up over too large an area before it could be joined and would blow or drip away.

Lasers can heat things up, but being a light beam rather than just heat they can be focused in to a tiny spot. A modest amount of heat, say a kilowatt in only a tiny spot a hundredth of an inch diameter is going to melt a spot of metal in thousandths of second and when it goes away the metal will freeze solid in a similar amount of time. Now the job was to get our two sheets of thin aluminum nearly in contact for perhaps a thousandth of a second, put our tiny spot of intense energy between them which would melt them both and crush them together before they froze. If we could do this properly we could weld these tubes at 10ft. per second. A $20 radiator was in site!

I hope you can follow this because I don't think I have ever encountered any job as fascinating.

When I got there the project had just been started. A large machine had been built which fed the two strips of metal together, it was not very rigid and was suspected of vibrating and spoiling the job. Quite a lot of my work was initially to get the whole machine stiffened up and the mirror mountings aiming the laser path rigidified or eliminated.

At first the one inch diameter laser beam needed these two mirrors to lower it to the work, so the work had to be raised about a foot to match the height of the very large laser machine, thus getting rid of the mirrors and their holding structure which was capable of shaking everything. This spoilt the aim of the final hot spot, which was only about one hundredth of an inch in diameter, but had the power of a medium size electric fire.

We tested the welds by immersing the tube in water and putting compressed air in it. When I started the tubes had about ten leaks per tube with occasional good welds. We got it down to perhaps two or three when the Great Blizzard of 77 struck. This was no trivial event. It has had at least one book written about it (not very literary).

It started Friday lunchtime, we were advised by management to go home immediately!! No such luck. I and several others set out for the car park. The plant buildings were laid out on a grid pattern, and were perhaps three storeys high. The first part of our walk was crosswind, quite sheltered although we didn't think so at the time. As we approached a left turn we stopped to watch a man on his knees on the ice being blown to the left at about 4m.p.h., the direction in which we hoped to walk. In conjunction with the snow we collectively decided not to try for home immediately.

The question of food came up. First all the candy machines were emptied. Later, since the entire canteen staff was caught like us, real meals began to appear. We now had to pass a dull evening playing moon landing games on our hand calculators. Various forms of insulation and padding were sought out, I never knew where they came from and we collectively slept til morning, which looked considerably less hazardous. There was sufficient snow to make travel doubtful, drifts behind houses could and did stretch across many roads. Son William walked up on to a roof! I managed to drive about two miles before facing reality, choice of direction was not available. The situation was so serious that the army was called in to help people marooned. People were found dead in cars. Fortunately the phone system stood up and once the overload eased up we all knew how we stood. I imposed myself on some kindly acquaintances who helped cheerfully. Second night out! Breakfast! Their newspaper was delivered. I found by phone that my home paper was also delivered so the inference was that I could drive to and from the newspaper office to get home. It was a varied ride including grocery store parking lots and novel one way streets but for the last two miles the road which had matched the wind direction exactly was totally clear and traveled at 50 m.p.h. Approximately 46 hours to get home from work.

Just about this time my sister-in-law in San Diego presented us with new nephew, her first, so Rosemary felt it incumbent on her to go and help. She flew from besieged Buffalo to San Diego, and as the aircraft circled to land, she had a feeling, prompted by the beaches and especially the palm trees, that we lived in the wrong place. (She had, after all, just driven home from the grocery store in snow with my daughter walking in front as a guide.) So... I followed my usual procedure and wrote to General Atomic in San Diego for a job and got a refusal.

Randy Hager a colleague of mine from the reprocessing plant which closed and Victor Barnhart who got me the one month profitable job in Pittsburg apparently remonstrated with them and I got a job. I left voluntarily for once but certainly not without some regrets. I was not able to check out my theory that air turbulence along the laser beam path was the last obstacle to the Union Carbide aluminum radiator.

My interview was rather fun. John Purcell, owner of a Cessna Twin and builder of the largest superconducting magnet ever, was one and John Alcorn, noted Battle of Britain historian the other. I don't think their interests misled them. I got to work, initially on a subscale model of the Russian fusion machine built to check out the line of theory. It checked out, but not before there was a certain amount of trouble with the stressing of the machine. It was tricky because some parts of the machine got progressively warmer as the machine cycled and the finite element programs available at that time didn't handle that. There was a very large version of the machine being built as well which needed work on the positioning of its instruments which could be sensitive to vibration and even to the mains alternating current. I had indications that the preliminary design work on this had been done by physicists! They had habits of cutting away major structures to get their instrumentation in. As an official sideline, resulting entirely from the background of my two interviewers, I was caught up in non atomic magnet applications. Big powerful superconducting magnets, which carry electrical current way beyond daily life, generate correspondingly large forces in addition to requiring operating temperatures near absolute zero. Commonly they need considerable structure just to hold together. In one notable case it was the earth.

I participated in an interesting earth supported study of a one mile diameter circular superconducting coil buried in a trench to take the enormous bursting forces, running alongside it was a similar amount of aluminium to absorb the heat generated in a potential accidental warm up. This coil could hold enough electrical energy to power a city for a few hours. Such a large vacuum container might well be a practical problem. Another job we looked at was energy storage for an aircraft carriers catapult, getting rid of the dangerous large steam lines of the conventional catapult, which had to run right through the ship and replacing them with a small car size engine.

Possibly the most intriguing jobs were the magnets for Magnetic Resonance Imaging which are medical diagnostic devices, not by superconducting standards very powerful, but useful immediately, (not always the case in research). In any superconducting magnet the job that requires most attention apart from the superconducting thing, is just supporting the magnetic coil in such a manner that heat does not seep in to the coil via its supports and stop it being superconducting. We designed a neat support through the vacuum space which kept the coil away from heat outside but conducted the minimum of heat in to the coil. My family has on occasion been a customer of MRI machines. One of the operators of a machine being used by my family told me that if by accident the coil of wire in the machine got heated to perhaps ten degrees above absolute zero it cost $30,000 to reset the machine! Just incidentally we accidentally did this in our workshop and filled the entire place with fog down to three feet above the floor since the cold helium froze the moisture in the air. We had to walk at a crouch.

Another thing I got in to was electric guns. Slightly against my principles but it was for the navy who lose a fair proportion of their ships in wartime from the explosion of their own ammunition. One of my schoolmasters was killed when H.M.S. HOOD blew up, sunk by one hit from the Bismark on her magazine. Electric guns have the interesting characteristic that given free reign, their maximum bullet speed is that of light, about 186,000 miles per second, quite a weapon. Very simple principals, you make a gigantic spark between two parallel copper rods and put a missile in front of it. The problem is that as well as the missile going forward the two copper rods try to fly apart at the same speed, and they need a great deal of restraint. The same principal lies behind the electric launch system for carrier aircraft. The plane is the bullet. The first electric guns were held together with rows of large bolts, both expensive and inconvenient. My trick avoided this fairly simply....But I was getting near retirement I thought.

John Purcell and I had during the previous four years, working two evenings and Saturday mornings engaged ourselves in the construction of an aeroplane. Inevitably with John involved it was unconventional, VW engine, two seats, two approximately equal wings only not one above the other as usual but one behind the other. The entire structure was foam and fiberglass. The front wing carried about 70% of the weight, elevator on the front wing and ailerons on the rear. Its performance was remarkable, top speed 140 MPH, 40 miles per gallon. It could be stalled, just, at about 60 MPH, when the nose dropped six inches, which it did on its own in the least rain. Very, very stable and a delight to fly except that with a slight lack of care it took 3000 ft, to land so you had better do it right. Ten MPH too fast and it took the entire airfield to stop. The VW engine as installed lacked trustworthiness. John was OK but I had an engine failure down wind, (vapor lock) and had to land with my son William copilot. My refusal to approach over water (in case we drowned) lead to an undercarriage repair. On the other occasion I had engine failure on takeoff. I turned round and landed safely since the plane could not be stalled!! This of course is in direct and absolute disobedience of the rule book but that was our plane. Superb design, bad engine (as installed). It was ignition failure of course. Amateur conversion of engines is rarely to be recommended. We were very courageous thinkers, we calculated that by filling the second seat with a shaped gasoline tank we could make the short Atlantic crossing. Fortunately we only thought about it.

If you mix any epoxy, depending on the total quantity, after about 15 minutes it will begin to heat up and set...so you have to be very careful to not mix more than you are ready to use or you will have your useful vessel filled permanently with expensive useless resin... or you can try to catch it before it becomes too stiff and use it up!! If many layers of fiberglass are needed you have to be careful to cover all except the last layer with a non bonding temporary cloth to roughen the surface to ensure bonding the next layer.

There are often many layers needed to get required strength. Its a small art, and not the only one.

John and I obviously worked the same hours so we had a slight problem in getting our numerous unusual orders for material delivered. Rosemary was the answer! Deliveries were made to our house. She got some amusing comments. Some of the foam blocks on which the plane was molded were enormous and virtually weightless and there were several sizes, not to mention buckets of resin, which weighed much more than enormous foam blocks. I think the delivery man thought we were nuts. Only the glasscloth was normal.

Sibley Burnett was my bosses boss although these relationships after working together for eleven years tended to become blurred. They both had relationships of a sort with the General Atomic owners who were actual aeroplane types having made exploratory flights into the Amazons in their youth. Both had made some money by investing in San Diego housing and factory space. They started off by getting me to modify the doorway of Sibleys giant hanger so they could move some overheight object. I did this almost without reference to the giant object. They then dispensed with that hanger and bought a much smaller one, more sensible. John, in his usual oblique way saw a use for single transistors, unusual since they are usually set up in vast batches, some cryogenic effort went in to that but ceased without notable outcome. They then came across a technical area which showed some potential.

The paper making industry had a problem. They could make the most beautiful white paper but after a few years it faded to a faint brownish yellow. Their customers for whatever reason preferred this not to happen. Even doping it with chalk produced negligable improvement. The cause apparently was iron and iron oxide, usually present in the process water in minute amounts. It all ended up as iron oxide which fortunately, even after oxidation retained some slight magnetism. This was it, superconducting magnets could fairly easily provide sufficient magnetism to pull it out. Of course you could do this but after a while the brown stuff accumulates around the magnet to the point where it fails to gather any more. Every so often you had to shut down the magnet and wash the iron oxide away. The problem was that when you shut off the magnet to let the oxide be flushed, the very considerable amount of heat created by the large energy content of the magnet boiled off all your expensive liquid helium. This would easily cancel out the exponential profit in selling the cleanest chalk in the world. This rogue heat would be deposited in the considerable amount of structural steel wound around the coil to hold it together, almost a perfect helium boiler.

What occurred to me was that you could probably have the superconductor in the helium and, with a bit of a trick, have the large amount of steel needed to keep it from bursting outside the helium vessel and insulated from it. The helium containement vessel could be only .036 inches thick with the tensile steel hardly in touch, insulated and outside the helium space. When the steel warmed up it would not be in contact with the helium.

We were lounging about collectively eating lunch when I mentioned this to the forum, Sibley leapt up to the phone and got hold of Don Brown, G.A.s ace welder and asked him what gauge was the thinnest stainless steel he could reliably weld. The answer, .028" delighted him because switching off a superconducting magnet without costing a fortune in liquid helium had hitherto been considered impossible. The others realised what it meant. Caused quite a stir!

I acquired the official status of consultant, flew monthly to San Diego, stayed in hotels and got a taste for Alaska Airlines lunch sandwiches. I nearly refused to come when, because of a political convention in San Diego my hotel price doubled! Sibley told me that the smallest expense account he had ever signed was my original one from Buffalo to San Diego. I obviously thought small. However when my grandson slept in the hotel with us at Rosemary's invitation he demonstrated that he at least had not inherited that tendency by asking where and when breakfast was. Not bad at four!

John and Sibley had one more shot to try before they quit. The conventional chalkfilter vessel had a diameter about ten times its thickness, it looked about like a very large fat quarter. Both to them and myself it seemed possible or even preferable that it should be half the diameter and twice as thick, obvious savings on magnet cost, steel cost and fabrication. The standard form was about ten feet in diameter and two feet thick. Well, work was started on this design. The draughtsman working on it was a most interesting character, an ex navy submariner with an interesting background. Amongst other things he was a member of family whose business produced a well recognised product, but who for the moment wanted do something else. As a submariner, during training he and his entire class had to remain underwater in a pool for one minute without aids. Then they had to surface. All the rest floated up. He was the only one dense enough to have to swim up! Not relevant to the story!

He and I over time became suspicious of this new filter vessel and thought that the internal flow in the magnetic field needed investigation. The "dumpier" vessel might focus the flow and mess up the entire concept. We thought that there should be some investigation of this. Very unfortunately we were proved right.

This left John and Sibley in a bad position. They could not afford to do it again, although we knew how and obviously the customer wanted his money back so the whole affair folded. As a retired person and a consultant all I had lost were the perks of being a consultant. But I was retired in a wonderful place.

We had with our small trailer camped at Sequim Wa. and found it congenial. On our second visit we explored the area somewhat. Rosemary wanted to go up this side road which "obviously" led nowhere. I agreed and there was, when we got there, much more than I thought... harbour, bookshop, cheap housing, airfield, beaches. Influenced probably by the fact that I didn't have to work it seemed the best place in the world. So we sold up in San Diego and moved in to a house near the Fairground, in Port Townsend, the best move we ever made. (and two cinemas!)

At first I didn't know about the Port Townsend model airplane club and so initially drove to Sequim, that is when I wasn't doing a bit of "private" model flying in the fairground opposite. I rigged a camera in my trainer model and photographed our house from the air, not a common feat in those days. Later

I joined the Sequim club, not surprisingly since I had an adventure in the fairground. I launched my model with a short power run but forgot to switch on the radio control. It climbed in a nice spiral until the engine stopped and then headed out across the lake. On the far side it lodged in a tree about 30 ft. up. No way to get it down I thought. However I saw an ad in the paper by a man who got cats down from trees at one dollar a foot, 30 dollars minimum. Nothing is impossible in Port Townsend... minus $30!

We found a sawn off tree stump on the beach, counted up to 900 rings.

There was a small airport at Port Townsend, I checked out in a Cessna 150 there. Not cheerful country to have engine trouble, however my checkout pilot was Lindbergs grandson. His significant comment was that everybody had a grandfather!

William James Bookshop was a treasure. Port Townsend apparently had people with similar tastes to ourselves all of whom bought and sold books, so we were never short of somewhere to go. There were two ice cream shops nearly opposite each other, one in an elevator... not working. And an excellent hardware store, not common by any means. I stopped by there one day for something and outside was a sporty car with the number MACH 30. I thought... not even the maddest road hog can boast that! The driver came out of the shop and approached the car, I said, "You must be one of those!" His reply was "Yes I Am"... My first and only astronaut, brought out the schoolboy in me. He told me that at that time there were about 90 of them all told including the Russians. He retired a couple of miles away in Port Ludlow. Nice town but a little bit "posh".

While we were in England one time Rosemary got a booklet published for book collectors. We were justified in reading this because when we moved we had 5700 lbs. of books according to the mover. There was a dealer in there who was specifically advertising to buy P.G. Wodehouse books. We had most of his works after about 1925. Rosemary had bought one book, with dust jacket at a garage sale during our more remote wanderings paying a whole dollar for it. So we wrote to this dealer telling him what we had. We knew the dust jacket on a 1926 anything would up its value. He said he would like to see it if we would send it, so we did. After all it was a P.G. Wodehouse. His offer was 1250 pounds sterling!!! (I bought an ordinary copy in its place, $6) We were going to England that year so we made an arrangement with our old Hiltingbury and Supermarine friends Brian and Sylvia Brown, and Penny Cawte who had lived there, to go to Paris. The journey itself was fun. We started at Waterloo and cruised gently to Dover at which point we became a "Train Grand Vitesse" and plunged under the English Channel. One goes past an oncoming train at such a speed that the entire event is one very loud short bang. We stayed in a small place in the Mairie and did tourist things including a visit to the Galleries Lafayette, Arc de Triomphe and the Tour Eifel. By the river we saw a man selling posters and one of a black cat caught our eye, being suitable as a present for our cat when we got home. But it was too large! Quelle Dommage! I still cannot believe that after about 60 years I was able to ask the man in French if he had a smaller version. He did!

Looking around at various possibilities Cyprus, at least the northern Muslim bit seemed attractive and after an internal debate we decided to give it a try and include Turkey. These were British organized tours, indeed we had to buy triple deckers first England then Instanbul then Northern Cyprus, the Muslim part of course. And we had to purchase the deal in Britain from the U.S. Instanbul impressed immediately and emphatically. We deliberately stayed in a non Western hotel to broaden our experience. It did show us the Turkish way of doing things, new to us and interesting. We did not entirely expect that since it was an older Turkish hotel, probably about one hundred years old, that it would be renovated nightly up to about nine o'clock, very loudly! The Instanbul market is immense and astonishingly varied, you can buy food and jewelry under the same roof! We did! And two Turkish carpets allegedly from the island in the Bosphorus but more probably worn out in Instanbul, not to mention a cigarette case made by Anders John Nevalainen, a Faberge employee. (U.S. dutiable!)

We moved on to Cyprus arriving at the airport to be met and taken to Kyrenia a port on the north shore, quite clearly at least medieval. We had rented a car and after a short orientation we picked it up. A generous description of the car would be ramshackle, almost expected on looking round, but the sticking throttle was a bit too much and the owner swapped it for his own on our complaint. We had a GPS, novel at the time so we went looking for ruins. They are not in the least dressed up for tourists as are most such things everywhere. They may indeed have remained thus since the Romans left. Quite a thrill, not tourist commonplace. One is also inspired to question the function of religion here. The people we met were very friendly without American/ European reserve, but there were Christian cemeteries all smashed up! And on Sundays Cypriots shoot birds!

There was a main dining room at the hotel where we ate which also had a smallish dance floor, running smoothly on Saturdays at least, and it was obvious that the local "Saturday Night Out" was to dine and dance here. Solid looking well dressed but not sombre people sitting at the tables. We danced a fair amount and thoroughly enjoyed ourselves at least partly because we could show off. No event could be more significant for Rosemary since a Cypriot gentleman wearing a very well tailored grey suit came to our table and, kissing Rosemary's hand said, "Madame, you dance beautifully" Wow!! Follow that.

We did. We went again. The journey was more adventurous than the first time, with some confusion at Instanbul at least when we left. Before that Rosemary got a strange rash never particularly debilitating which may have vanished of its own accord in spite of treatment. We did the Istanbul things including visiting the Hadji Sophia, a vast Christian cathedral converted to Muslim with a spectacular stone arch roof supported on giant columns, known locally as "elephants feet", about ten feet in diameter. We had a look at the more modern district, just that, and visited the ferry across the Golden Horn and the chariot racing track, inevitably defunct and then took off for Nicosia again. We were obviously the last aircraft in to that airport that night. Our luggage was not on the flight! It became very dark. We were met by two pleasant fellows each driving a car, one for us and one for them. Obviously I had been along that road twice before, it was narrow, unlit, had ill defined edges, steep in parts and was curvaceous on the mountainous bits. The surface wasn't too good either. I said I didn't want to do it so the two lads drove one car each and we got to our destination, without luggage, safely. We found out that in the absence of luggage the immediate and prominent deficiency is lack of soap! However our luggage was present when we first appeared the next morning so we didn't have to buy clothes. By the way there was no electricity that night! The place had changed considerably since our last visit, new guest buildings and much tidying up and perhaps we were caught up in this.

This time we could take a little more risk with the car. We went west from Kyrenia to Salamis, an amazing complex of ruins with mosaic floors and entirely residual walls, obviously important and probably a one time palace. It was very high, emphasized by the fact that it stood virtually on a clifftop, and several thousand square feet in area with colored mosaic floor. Once again there was no attempt at preservation or protection of the site. On the North side was a sheer cliff to the empty sea, and on the south side difficult parking for several cars. It is probable that there are opportunities for archaeological excavation here as in so many places on the island.

Along this road, several miles from Kyrenia was a surprising sight, an almost perfect English suburban house with a ground floor shop stocked adequately with what you might expect to find plus a good amount of local tourist trade goods. It was so English and brand new as to be at the limit of belief, Dad shopkeeper, wife and two children. The couple had lived in England in a perfectly usual way when dad inherited a Cypriot legacy of some substance, including this land. The whole family was full of enthusiasm, the children came in from exploration and said they had found a fluted column in the bush. I can't imagine what eventually happened to this enterprise, the setup was completely perfect with one exception. There was absolutely no indication in Kyrenia that such an attractive facility existed. They were six or seven miles out of town on a marginal road. They treated us very kindly, the shop was not nominally open for a day or two. We were and are saddened, a perfect setup in the wrong place.

The other drive we did was east on the long road to the monastery at the eastern tip of Cyprus but after fifteen miles of dirt road without sight of another vehicle we decided the monastery at the eastern tip, although nearly at Palestine was too isolated. We didn't see another vehicle.

One evening when there was no dancing in the room where Rosemary had her hand kissed we were rather solemnly eating our evening meal when a very well dressed gang of young people arrived, sat down at a table which was laid out for them and started a merry party. They soon noticed us quietly in the background and decided we didn't match their cheery birthday party so we were invited to join in. They were highly europeonised folks from Instanbul, spoke English and were travel agents. The party including us was about twelve. The men did some amazing Cossack dancing, in properly tailored suits, (!) one was from Chechna, and the ladies were probably Greek since they were all exceptionally good looking.

Nicosia is in the centre of Cyprus and because of the historic inability of the Greeks and Turks to get on, (the British who stopped them fighting had left,) as the capital it boasted a "Berlin Wall". We found our way through it and wandered round not noticing a lot of difference. We came across a building in which there were genuine "Whirling Dervishes". We thought they were mythical! A spectacular sight in their spinning white, conical habits.

We were interested in traveling by ship, unlike conventional vacations you have to do a minimum of work but find a great many non work interesting things to do. The first cruise we took was to Norway, from Southampton of course, in the Caronia. The need for oil was the first thing that was visible to us since the ship passed a few miles from a working oil rig in the North Sea. Nothing else was in sight, very lonely. We sailed on to fjords, some with glaciers at their head one of which "calved" as we watched. The ship was only certified for a certain size of floating ice so we could not go too near. We passed by the place where the wartime German heavy water plant was, and the raid took place which destroyed it and we saw seven waterfalls at once. If Cunard ever need a salesman for this cruise I will do it for expenses.

There was a sightseeing flight we could take, a chance to ride behind a radial engine in a de Havilland Beaver, too much to resist. So we stood in line and were allocated a big Cessna!! but we had a laugh anyway. A small very aggressive lady said she would sit next to the pilot and pushed to the front. I just smiled... after a short while the pilot arrived and started loading. He sat the aggressive lady in the rear seat and unfortunately my wife in the other rear seat. I knew this would happen. Any pilot of a small plane puts his heaviest client in the front and the lightest in the back, or he can spend ten revenue minutes doing the weight and balance calculation for that flight. If he knows the passenger weights! He put me in the front! The takeoff was the roughest ride I've ever had in an aircraft. We crossed the wake of a smallish boat and each wave of the wake gave such an impact I thought we were bound to be in trouble. After that it was peaceful with a light rain which diluted the visibility somewhat, still spectacular however.

We went up a mountain, riding in a cable car and in the course of standing in the inevitable queue we found ourselves in the line with the captain of our ship, his wife and two daughters. Naturally enough we each enquired where the other came from. They were English and said they lived near Niagara Falls so we naturally guessed Lewiston (we knew very well that it was near the Falls). We were wrong, his view of "near" included Williamsville. Our son called it "Myville" since the age of three.

Later we went to a market. Typical things were for sale in an urban market, some souvenirs plus several stalls selling the ultimate sweater for me! Never mind that I live in San Diego! This of course was high summer and in spite of the overcast and slight tendency to drizzle very many outdoor tables at restaurants were occupied which gave one a strange feeling... is this real?

The other place of note that we saw was Narvik fjord, best described as narrow and solemn. My goodness it was pretty sombre. It was quite clear that a combination of Norwegian weather and that geography would have given the RAF a tricky bombing job. (you have to be old to follow that)

One of the cleverer things you can do when you retire is to find somewhere that suits you and has much more reasonable living costs, this we had done to perfection. Port Townsend met that criterion and then some, so we could indulge in cruises and visits to exotic places to a modest extent. However we had a family misfortune after some years of feeling pretty free and felt it was incumbent on us to return to San Diego which at least partially reversed that effect. But not before we had caroused about some more.

So a trip to the Mediterranean to see a total eclipse of the sun was, to my delight achievable. We got to Livorno to board an Italian vessel, right near Pisa but the Leaning Tower was not included, goodness knows why. There was a professional grade rainstorm when we arrived by bus at the dock, but we, by which I mean the cruise guests were all sheltered. (This subsequently seemed out of character.) But it wasn't dull, we saw crowds of people arriving in pouring rain! It took three hours to get on board and we were immediately both stricken with sickness as were some hundred and fifty visitors. This sounds like a considerable complaint but it was an adventure rewarded. The efficiency of the tiny medical (and cleaning) staff in dealing with the unpleasantness was unbelievable. They came upon you like a tornado, brief injection and advice, crowd of cleaners, and by dinner time it was merely remembered with astonishment, an aspect of the medical profession I have not seen before or since. Broader application of their methods would result in more immortality.

Our cabin was unusual, there was little interruption of the shower water flowing from the shower floor to most of the rest of the cabin, no sill but somehow we persisted in enjoying ourselves. Italians apparently have the ability to be industrious and relaxed at the same time.

We wandered into the ballroom one day and there was a dance competition going on. I would have described it as of medium quality, no geniuses (?), no shufflers, a few creditable dancers and no American style. It was daytime so there was a large audience. We gazed at this for a while as always fascinated by the lower echelons. We watched and after some thought decided we could be valid competitors so we joined in. Oh dear, judging was by acclamation!!

And we came in second. To our gratification several people said the winners only won because they were Italian, local favoritism!

We stopped in Naples but only to look at Vesuvius. There was a bus which ground its way to the top. Quite a sound looking road but when we got there we saw the remains of the funicular as featured in the well known opera. Set up by Thomas Cook! The guides didn't mention it, I could not believe my eyes. The crater was an enormous hemispherical pit, half a mile across and steaming gently at the bottom. The entire content of that half mile hemisphere had, at one time been blown into the atmosphere. Ones level of self confidence diminished perceptibly, but the fear was forgotten as we passed through the Sicilian Straits next day.

Apart from the eclipse the major event of this trip was going to Alexandria, starting point for the most packed day of cruising ever, although they usually get a lot in. We had about a two hour bus ride to get to the picture book Egypt. We had a very erudite guide who unfortunately spent the whole trip expounding on the history, which one could read and nothing about what could be seen, which is as impressive as you can imagine. To anybody who has been near civil engineering the whole place is impossible. It is no longer permitted to climb any of the multiple pyramids, the big one would be a days job. The sphinx however is smaller than I expected, but the assembly, to really use a hackneyed phrase, is awesome. Rosemary I'm glad to say was photographed on a camel (for a fee). In view of the considerable mix of races and nations present there were policemen about. They were discreet and spectacular simultaneously if such a thing is possible. They could be seen a few hundred yards away, mounted on camels and with a rifle slung about the harness. Movies get it right! We got a lot of experience on this trip, including going underground to see carved walls. We rode back to the place where there were facilities for coaches, food etc. on camels. These poor beasts have a reputation for being malodorous, my opinion is that given competition they would tie with the horse. Getting on one however is an adventure, you are almost certain you are going over the front since they get up back end first.

We rode back to the ship by a partially urban route and were able to see an Egyptian version of traffic congestion. The first and most obvious thing was the absence of emission restrictions on vehicles. It was similar to Buffalo in the seventies, quite homely. However the most striking thing was the apparent neglect of the most elementary safety measures. There was no evidence of seat belts anywhere, worn or otherwise. Men traveled at forty miles per hour seated on the back of flat bed trucks, smoking of course with their legs hanging over the sides and no restraint whatever, and there was general exterior strap hanging, one bump and there would be bodies everywhere. But apart from normal noise the atmosphere was incredibly relaxed. Any where else the people would look terrified. Even the cyclists looked undisturbed and the whole mass moved past them at about 40 M.P.H.

We sailed out next morning to pick up the trail of the total eclipse which ran due west along the central Mediterranean. People began to gather on deck with all kinds of apparatus from eclipse glasses which are a more intense version of sunglasses to small telescopes with filters and elaborate cameras. There was plenty of room for everybody, the trick was to find a hatch to sit on while you waited. We did and were next to a couple with what was obviously their grandaughter. We got in to conversation which, since nobody was near home, started with finding out where each came from. I don't recall where the couple came from but their daughter came from Poway in California, very near our daughter and son in law. So we asked where she went to school and it was the same school as our grandson, and she knew him! She said, in hushed tone-"but he's the school president" We didn't know the pupils were given such exalted status! We saw the whole total eclipse which was ideal and not by any means always the case, cloud can play the devil! We saw Jupiter and several brighter stars as well, having a clear view since the sun was almost directly overhead. The technical contingent were well pleased. We also had a bonus on this already relatively long event in that the ship, many of whose passengers had come specifically for this, ran at speed down the track prolonging an already generous event by a few seconds. We sailed on to Larnaca in southern Cyprus. The similarity to Bexhill on Sea in England was positively depressing, all it needed was a little rain. We got home all right!

Many or perhaps most of our European trips were made easy by the kindness of my brother John and his wife Susan, talented and efficient. Whenever we went on a trip which started in England they welcomed us back, which gave us opportunity to visit all the locations associated with our first house and the neighbourhood we lived in when we were first married, not to mention that Southampton is a good cruise port. Susans version of an English tea restores the soul of an exile. John too has a magical connection to Heathrow, He knows how to get in AND out. Once when in Chandlers Ford I went to visit my old firm, Selwoods. They had certainly heard of me (25 years later!), but the atmosphere was that of a car showroom. They hired equipment out and sold it. Glossy leaflets and all, just like a car showroom, no mud.

We had of course spent a lot of effort on mostly European travel, and felt we might balance this up a little. We saw a crazy cheap offer to go to New Zealand, we found out why it was cheap in due course but nonetheless it was value for money. It was only for a week, there was a free car rental for three days, the cost of the car for the remainder of the week was what you might expect if you suffer from basic cynicism. We also paid somewhat for food, except at Macdonalds where we found out that, with purchase or not, coffee was free to seniors! We do not however have any regrets. We lost October 3rd on the way out, fun but disappointing as the 4th is my birthday and of course it was our longest flight ever, about seventeen hours. We only saw the North island, regretted not seeing more but certainly got what we paid for. The hotel was modest and bore none of the indefinable distinction of England where pre and post war still seems to infiltrate everything. However there was definitely an English feeling, rather strange when we could immerse ourselves in a volcanically heated hot tub. The ground was definitely and palpably warm in places, fortunately without any active vulcanism. The local people don't seem to think about that possibility although we saw meals being cooked in hot boxes on the ground. We did buy an empty bottle clearly of originally square form which was considerably distorted by the heat, having been buried. We went to where the ferry for the south island left, walked on warm ground and saw a long beach entirely of black sand. We wondered why there were no freeways round Wellington until we drove about a little. There was no need! Seventeen hours home.

If you live in San Diego the Caribbean and Hawaii tend to have diminished attraction in relation to other destinations. We did however go to our friends in Florida, more to see them than Florida and the alligators. Aside from the pleasure of seeing them we were astonished by the fact that a continuous stream of Boeing 747's at the airport is only just capable of filling and emptying the cruise ships using Miami on Saturdays. Aeronautics were the main event apart from the visit. We went to an airport where there were rides available in a 1928 biplane. I am ashamed to say that I cannot recall its type but it had a "two holer" cockpit, the front one being big enough for two people... Rosemary and I! The plane was older than one of us. The third airport we visited (we did stay with our friends) was a privately owned one with a truly astonishing collection of aircraft and parts. An approximately fifteen foot by thirty foot wall of one hanger was a rack filled with antique acro engines. That hanger had a fairly wide paved apron in front of it, on which the airport owner was showing off the incredible performance of the German Feiseler Storch, by landing, stopping and taking off continuously *in front of* the hanger. I have seen many model aircraft that could not do that. With things like that what was a beach for?

The feeling prevailed that we should "do" the Panama Canal, eastbound as it happened.

Los Angeles happened to be the starting point and our first stop, for no discernible reason was Ensenada in Mexico. We did not go ashore, our angelinos may have done but we figured it might be a bit like Tijuana. It was apparent that there was a considerable fishing industry there. Cabo San Lucas????????? was our next port, giant rocks in the sea and a self sufficient air, none of that "suburb of Los Angeles" feeling, it looked and felt European, complement or otherwise. It also had all the look and feel of a Hollywood movie set which seems apparently to get the atmosphere right. So we liked it! We got a taxi driver who said he would take us all day for $30 if we went to where he recommended lunch. Well we did, it was a real enjoyable bargain. We had a long lunch watching the Mexican cliff diver lads, truly spectacular, the highest dive must be at least 100 feet. It was clear you had better hit the water cleanly or you could get seriously hurt, and don't hit a fellow diver. There was opportunity to see they were rewarded for such a spectacular show. A true highlight, the taxi driver had an easy day and we had a definite Mexican event.

Next we stopped at a small village about half way down the isthmus in Costa Rica, Puntarenus, where the people seemed pretty poor, but where there was for sale an amazing range of pottery. I think they were getting some form of assistance. The pots were wonderful but the one we wanted was sold just too soon. When you see what you like don't hesitate too long.

I had always imagined that the entrance to the canal would be a sort of indentation in perhaps a somewhat rural coast. I was surprised until I remembered that Panama is a place where unusual financial transactions are possible, presumably accounting for the skyscrapers. There must be a lot of them.

Massive concrete works were the first impression of the canal, commonplace if there are big ships around. Although I have actually walked under the Queen Mary this was no less impressive, everything is large, the ships fill this massive trough with a foot or two to spare. The designers decision on the width and depth of the canal must have been weighty. There are locks to stop the oceans rushing from one side to the other as the levels are rarely the same and where changes in level are needed there are giant electric tugs to move the ships through the locks. Wherever there was engineering there was an impression of well run order, but it wasn't all technical. Considerable lengths of the canal resemble a river, not surprisingly since the canal itself has small rivers flowing into it. This means that the canal is basically fresh water so needs to be that much deeper. The rivers and canal have smallish trees growing alongside them, dense but not very high for some distances, the impression is more rural than industrial. It is a sobering thought that this innocent looking scene originally killed hundreds of workers with yellow fever, causing the project to be abandoned at first attempt. In some places the soil is such that the canal is slowly filling in with landslips needing constant dredging.

Eventually we emerged into open water and turned west to head to Cartagena, a very beautiful place but it was so hot that we gave up with real regret after an hour or so and returned to the ship. We saw most beautiful Spanish style houses, and were accosted by a group of small Columbian boys waving "weapons" that had us thoroughly confused for a moment until a stranger explained that we were apparently involved in some historical tradition. At first we really wondered what was going on. Juvenile bandits?

We sailed past the island of Mustique but it looked much like other islands. Not easy to justify the hotel rate which was $1,500 per day... there were similar islands.

About this time we heard that the Queen Mary 2 was entering service and since we had been on the last service crossing of the original, we decided to get in on the new one, Last Westbound, first Eastbound. New York made sure the event was noticed! There were helicopters, police boats complete with bow mounted machine guns, searchlights, fireworks, helicopters, music and lots of small craft buzzing about. There were crowds of people, a nice indication of the affection New Yorkers had for Cunard after over a century of collaboration. A very sentimental journey, but this time we had no children with us. The crew called a meeting of anybody who had been on the last crossing of the first Queen Mary. There were four of us, ourselves, a young lad who must have been very young first time and a lady who originally had the benefit of a nanny, whom she evaded to escape into Tourist Class which was much more fun, only she had a lot of trouble finding her way back and had to call for the crews help. One assumes her parents had frantic reactions. If you wish to relax ocean crossings are much more restful than cruises.

Aside from all the good times I have had I have often wondered why there is an enormous volume of writing which is the subject of study, criticism and public interest and adulation or even condemnation.

What is obvious to me is that the first human requirement is to eat and a substantial proportion of the worlds population seem to be short in that respect. That is naive and unfortunately almost disastrously truthful. The modern way of dealing with innovation is to bury it in company records and only infrequently to push the thing forward to actual patent, resulting in the burial of due credit and a lack of status of the technical pioneer.

If for instance the names Shakespeare and Parsons with their achievements were by magic eliminated from human activity, what would be the result? No airliners, no electricity, and probably a few other penetrating deficiencies including a disastrous disablement of food supply. And Parsons is only one of thousands, including the inventor of the tin opener who are without honor.

Printed in the United States
By Bookmasters